ISBN 9781739490331

Cover design by Ricardo Sorzano and Kieran Trestain

Interior design by Ricardo Sorzano and Kieran Trestain

Produced in the United Kingdom

Acknowledgments:

We extend our heartfelt gratitude to our families for their unwavering support and encouragement during the writing process. We could not have completed this book without their constant love and understanding. We would like to thank the following individuals who helped with the read-throughs of the early material, providing us with invaluable feedback and perspective that greatly improved the book.

- Jonathan Yakeen
- Kyle Ahmed
- Liban Ali-Jama
- Elijah Tafari Johnson
- Bethany Latrece
- Tony Weeks
- Trudy Wrake
- Kaiden Trestain
- Kaila Trestain

Downloadable Resources:

The 15-Year Plan has an invaluable companion, in the online digital resource guide. As you embark on this transformative journey of envisioning and planning for your future, this guide is your trusted companion, offering an array of tools, templates, and ongoing support. It has been thoughtfully curated to empower you in crafting a vision for personal and professional growth that is both attainable and fulfilling.

Within these pages, you'll discover a diverse range of resources, each tailored to specific facets of your long-term plan. But this is just the beginning. Our commitment to your success extends beyond this guide. You can anticipate a wealth of additional materials, including documents, Excel spreadsheets, and even video content, all designed to provide you with continuous guidance and support. These assets are designed to enhance your understanding and application of the strategies, ensuring a more comprehensive and engaging learning experience.

PREFACE: PHILOSOPHY BEHIND THE FRAMEWORK ..i

Do You Know Where You Stand? ii

Frameworks For A Purposeful Life iv

Before We Dive In..vii

CHAPTER 1: PERSONAL AUDITING 3

Personal Audit 4

Self-Assessment 5

Personal Audit Prompts 7

Identifying Skills 17

Bench Marking 19

Skills Assessment Rating System 20

Skill Categories 21

Pro Tip: Transferable Skills 24

Chapter Summary 25

CHAPTER 2: DEFINING YOUR VISION 27

Determining Your Vision... 28

Step 1: Identify What Matters Most 28

Step 2: Envision Your Ideal Future 29

Step 3: Set Bold And Inspiring Goals 31

Embracing Bucket List Goals 33

Pro Tip: The Decision-Making Framework 35

Chapter Summary 37

CHAPTER 3: PHASES 39

Phases 40

Grounding The Phases.. 41

Make It Measurable And Time-Bound 44

Seek Support And Accountability............................. 49

Adapt And Review Regularly 51

Pro Tip: The Priority Pyramid...52

Chapter Summary 55

A New Phase...57

CHAPTER 4: FINANCIAL HEALTH **61**

Financial Health..62

The Distinction Between Salary, Revenue, And Income............63

Action Plan For Financial Prudence 64

Debt Management 67

Diversifying Income..68

Tax Planning 70

Retirement Planning 71

Legacy Planning 72

Chapter Summary 74

CHAPTER 5: DEVELOPING YOUR PERSONAL BRAND IDENTITY **77**

Developing Your Personal Brand 78

Pro Tip: Public Perception And Reputation 81

Imposter Syndrome..83

Overcoming Imposter Syndrome 84

Pro Tip: Brand Voice 85

Pro Tip: Shop Window 86

Chapter Summary 88

CHAPTER 6: BULIDING YOUR NETWORK **90**

The Essence Of Networking 91

The Network Tier List 92

Network Auditing..93

Pro Tip: The Perception Puzzle - Shaping Your Image In Other Networks 98

Characters In Your Network 100

Chapter Summary 102

CHAPTER 7: EFFECTIVE CONVERSATIONS MASTERY 105

Effective Conversations Mastery 106

The Four Pillars: Context, Emotion, Perspective, Resolution 107

Context: The Keystone Of Understanding 108

Emotion Intelligence: Guiding Your Emotional Navigation...... 109

Pro Tip: The Significance Of Active Listening 111

Resolution: Navigating Toward Shared Ground 112

Chapter Summary 114

CHAPTER 8: NAVIGATING SETBACKS 117

Continuous Improvement 118

The Art Of Continuous Self-Updating 118

Failing Successfully 120

The Power Of Perspective 121

Shaping The Image Of Failure 121

Negative Lenses That Can Colour The Image Of Failure........ 122

Perception Of Competition.. 123

Extracting Lessons From Failure................................ 124

Resilience And Perseverance 125

Pivoting Successfully 126

Pro Tip: Force Majeure 130

Chapter Summary 131

CONCLUSION.. 133

AFTERWORD 135

PREFACE:
PHILOSOPHY BEHIND
THE FRAMEWORK

Do You Know Where You Stand?

In today's fast-paced world, where instant gratification and ever-accelerating changes dominate our daily lives, the prospect of planning 15 years for greatness might appear daunting. It's no secret that many individuals find themselves trapped in mundane jobs, lacking opportunities for growth and personal development.

Indeed, time is a precious resource, and 15 years might seem like a significant portion of our lives, far in the future and in today's climate many may see the future as unstable or bleak. Yet, when we consider the vast array of opportunities, growth, and accomplishments that can be attained during this period, and the multitude of opportunities that portion of time grants us to succeed, the significance of 15 years becomes evident.

The world increasingly favours quick fixes and instant success, the concept of dedicating time to plan your life for greatness may feel counterintuitive. The allure of shortcuts and immediate rewards often tempts individuals to opt for short-term gains rather than committing to long-term visions. However, true greatness seldom emerges from fleeting endeavours.

Greatness takes time. Significant, sustained achievements and meaningful impact are rarely the result of impulsive actions or short bursts of effort. Rather, they are the product of strategic planning, steadfast dedication, and precise execution over an extended timeframe.

The key lies in the intent and purposefulness of our planning and actions. Outside of work alone, to build anything of meaning in life requires alignment with your core, with the things that truly motivate you to continue to change, adapt and plug away in a highly saturated global system.

Across the next few years, will see more advanced to our way of living than ever before, that will require different skills than the past. This is an important opportunity to embrace a continuous journey of improvement and growth. We can acquire new skills, build meaningful relationships, and learn from both successes and setbacks. The journey is not linear, but with the progress made day by day, the seemingly small and incremental step accumulates into something extraordinary over time.

Imagine the boundless possibilities that arise when we wholeheartedly embrace, the journey we were born for. You become unshakable to outside influences as you understand what each step you make is leading towards. Across this timeframe, we have the chance to leave a profound mark on our chosen path, our community, or even the world. You may start pioneering innovative ideas, challenging the status quo, and inspiring others through your own unwavering perseverance and dedication to your plan.

Let us remember that greatness is not attained by chance. It demands a deliberate effort to stay on course, maintain unwavering focus, and consistently take the right steps. Greatness requires us to push beyond our comfort zones, embrace change, and continually refine our approach. So, instead of viewing 15 years as an eternity, let us embrace it as an incredible opportunity for planning a life full of purpose.

Just as a business plan lays the foundation for a thriving company, a 15-Year Plan serves as the blueprint for a fulfilling and purposeful life. It is a comprehensive approach that recognizes the significance of long-term vision, strategic thinking, and adaptability to navigate the complexities of life. By approaching our lives with the same level of planning and intentionality that successful businesses do, we unlock the potential for growth, resilience, and meaningful achievements.

In business, adaptability is vital to survive in a constantly evolving marketplace. Similarly, life presents us with unpredictable twists and turns, demanding our ability to adapt and pivot. A well-structured Plan acknowledges the need for flexibility. It breaks down long-term goals into manageable phases, providing room to adjust our course based on changing circumstances, opportunities, and personal growth. Embracing this adaptability empowers us to stay true to our vision while making necessary adjustments along the way.

The 15-Year Plan: Frameworks for a Purposeful Life is not a quick fix or a one-size-fits-all solution. Instead, it is a guide that allows you to delve deep into the core of your being, challenging you to confront your fears, uncover your true potential, and make intentional choices aligned with your values and aspirations. It offers practical exercises, thought-provoking insights, and real-life examples to support you on your transformative journeys.

We understand that such a long timeframe may seem daunting. However, breaking down your life into phases allows you to prioritize, compartmentalize, and work on both the long-term vision and the short-term milestones. It provides you with the opportunity to reflect, evaluate, and adjust your course along the way, ensuring that you remain focused and aligned with your evolving aspirations.

It is our hope that within these words, you will find inspiration, guidance, and the reassurance that you are not alone on this journey. We have all stood where you stand now, filled with questions, seeking direction, and yearning for a life of purpose and meaning. This book is our offering to you, a roadmap to navigate the complexities of the modern world and uncover the limitless possibilities that await.

Embrace the opportunity to know where you stand, for it is from this foundation that you will begin to build the life you desire. May this serve as a gentle nudge, reminding you that the power to transform your life lies within your hands.

Frameworks For A Purposeful Life

The 15-Year Plan Framework is a comprehensive approach designed to help individuals navigate their journey towards long-term success and fulfilment. It is built on the belief that intentional and strategic planning, combined with continuous learning and personal development, can lead to profound transformations and significant achievements. It recognizes that success is not a linear path but a dynamic process that requires balance, resilience, and flexibility. By setting long-term goals, prioritizing, and cultivating the right mindset, individuals can take charge of their lives and create a meaningful impact.

Each chapter will provide unique frameworks, which is designed to address common challenges faced by individuals seeking personal and professional growth. Collectively these different frameworks provide the different tools that build and support your growth over a 15-year period. It combines elements of goal setting, self-assessment, continuous learning, networking, and adaptability to create a holistic approach that aligns with your values and aspirations. By embracing this framework, you will be empowered to overcome obstacles, seize opportunities, and make purposeful decisions that lead to long-term success.

The Underlying Thinking That The 15-Year Plan Is Rooted In, Boils Down To Eight Core Principles:

- ❖ Self-Awareness
- ❖ Clarity
- ❖ Phased Success
- ❖ Financial Health
- ❖ Personal Brand Cultivation
- ❖ Synergy Within Your Network
- ❖ Crafting Meaningful Interactions
- ❖ Resilience

Self-Awareness - Personal Auditing: Explore the depths of self-awareness through a comprehensive personal audit. Understand your unique strengths, values, and aspirations, laying the foundation for your transformative journey.

Clarity - Defining Your Vision: Craft a powerful Blueprint that paints a vivid picture of your desired future. define your goals, dreams, and aspirations, allowing your vision to guide your actions and decisions throughout the 15-year plan.

Financial Health – Supporting Your Ambitions: Expanding on the solid base of financial Literacy, you can ensure a thriving and sustainable future, fully realizing the possibilities of your long-term goals.

Phased Success - Achieving Your Goals In Stages: Utilize the concept of phased success, breaking down your long-term vision into manageable phases. Set specific, measurable, and time-bound goals for each phase, ensuring steady progress, and celebrating achievements along the way.

Personal Brand Cultivation - Grow Your Brand: Nourish and develop your personal brand, showcasing your unique identity, values, skills, and expertise. Craft an authentic and compelling narrative that leaves a lasting impression, opening doors to new opportunities.

Synergy Within Your Network - Optimizing Your Network For Success: Harness the power of synergy within your network. Cultivate meaningful connections and surround yourself with supportive individuals who align with your vision and values. Build a network that uplifts and empowers you, unlocking collaborative opportunities for growth and success.

Crafting Meaningful Interactions - Effective Conversation Mastery: Step into the position of a communicative master, through unique frameworks that connect the threads of daily conversation, to weave a tapestry of understanding and meaningful connection on your 15-year journey.

Resilience - Navigating Setbacks: Embrace resilience as a guiding principle in navigating setbacks. View setbacks as valuable learning opportunities and catalysts for growth. Develop the ability to adapt, persevere, and overcome challenges, emerging stronger and more determined on your path to success.

These frameworks are not a rigid set of rules, but a flexible roadmap tailored to your unique circumstances and aspirations. It provides a structure that guides you through the key aspects of personal and professional growth.

Throughout this book, you will explore various concepts and strategies that form the pillars of the 15-Year Plan. You will learn how to define a compelling vision that guides your actions, develop a personal brand that sets you apart, build a supportive network that fuels your growth, and take consistent action while tracking your progress.

Additionally, you will discover the importance of continuous learning and improvement, embracing a growth mindset, and adapting to change as you navigate the ever-evolving landscape of personal and professional growth. Each chapter will provide valuable insights, practical exercises, and real-life examples to illustrate how the principles of the framework can be applied to your own journey. Remember, this plan is not a rigid blueprint but a flexible roadmap. It allows for customization and adjustment based on your individual circumstances, interests, and goals. It is a tool to help you create a roadmap for the next set of years, filled with purpose, growth, and fulfilment.

As you embark on this transformative journey, we encourage you to approach it with an open mind, a willingness to embrace change, and a commitment to personal growth. These frameworks are designed to empower you to take control of your life, make conscious choices, and create a future that aligns with your true potential.

Before We Dive In

Before we dive into the core content, we want to acquaint you with the structure of this book. It is divided into two distinct phases, each playing a crucial role in your personal growth and development.

Part 1: Laying The Groundwork

In this initial part, we will guide you through the process of visualizing your ideal life. We want you to envision a life filled with purpose, meaning, and fulfilment. However, before we can build on this vision, we need to get to establish a solid foundation. This means auditing and understanding your current circumstances, beliefs, and values. By exploring your present reality, you will gain a clear understanding of where you currently stand.

During this section, we will help you identify any obstacles or limitations that might be holding you back. We will encourage you to reflect on your strengths, weaknesses, and the core values that define you. By understanding these aspects, you will be able to create a solid foundation upon which you can build the life you desire.

Part 2: From Vision To Reality

Once you have gained clarity and laid your foundation in Part 1, it's time to act. In this second section, we will provide you with a practical roadmap to bring your vision to life. You will learn actionable steps, strategies, and techniques to help you navigate the path towards your goals.

We firmly believe that your dreams are within reach, and it's time for you to aim high. Together, we will explore various methods to overcome obstacles, develop resilience, and cultivate the mindset necessary to pursue your ambitions.

Throughout this book, we will provide guidance, encouragement, and support to empower you on this incredible journey. Remember, building a purposeful life is a process that requires commitment, effort, and dedication. Embrace the lessons, embrace the challenges, and embrace the opportunity to transform your life.

Now, let us embark on this remarkable expedition together. Get ready to visualize, strategize, and take action as we guide you towards a life of purpose and fulfilment. Let's begin.

PART 1: LAYING THE GROUNDWORK

CHAPTER 1:
PERSONAL AUDITING

Personal Audit

Clarity is something many of us yearn for—a deeper understanding of ourselves and a clearer path to follow. However, the process of discovering what truly drives us is far from simple. As children, we approach life with curiosity and innocence, but as we transition into adulthood, our experiences and the influence of society begin to shape our beliefs, habits, and values. These ingrained patterns often become so deeply rooted that they obscure our true essence and may hinder us from progressing through life with a deep curiosity, that we are all born with.

Within the 15-year plan the Personal Audit emerges as the initial transformative tool in creating a purposeful life. This Audit is designed to take you back to your ground zero, providing a detailed examination of the areas of your life that shape your identity and determine your future. Through thought-provoking questions and introspective exercises, this process prompts you to engage in deep reflection and radical transparency. It challenges you to confront your beliefs, values, passions, and aspirations in an honest and authentic way.

When embarking on your journey, it is important to remember that your starting point does not reflect your full potential. Through a thorough personal audit, you can assess your current abilities and identify areas for growth. It is crucial to understand that this audit is merely a snapshot of your journey so far and where you are at a given moment and should not define who you can become. Your starting point could be at a negative place, but with ambition, determination, and self-belief, you have the power to transform and surpass any limitations. There is no cap on growth and development. Embrace the fact that your personal and professional capacity can expand exponentially, from negative to a million, and beyond. It all depends on your inner drive and commitment to the journey.

Courage and a willingness to be vulnerable are required as you confront both the triumphs and the challenges that have shaped your path. Through this deep exploration, you gain invaluable insights into your true desires, strengths, and areas for growth. The path may not always be easy, but with each step, you move closer to living a life that is truly aligned with your deepest values and aspirations.

Self-Assessment

As you take your first steps towards introspection, it is crucial to allocate dedicated time and space to delve into the key areas that form your foundation. Prepare yourself to embark on this introspective quest by setting aside a few hours of solitude. Find a quiet space where you can be free from distractions and create an atmosphere conducive to deep reflection. Arm yourself with a journal or a notebook and a pen, as you will embark on a journey of self-exploration, capturing your thoughts, insights, and reflections along the way.

Within the pages of your journal, you will navigate through various aspects of your life getting to the heart of what makes you tick. The prompts and questions are there to help you think about what's important to you, the lens you perceive the world through, and what your goals are. This is a down-to-earth, honest look at yourself, aiming to bring clarity and focus to your everyday decisions and long-term plans.

Remember, this is an intensely personal and important process. It is an opportunity to reconnect with your core essence, rediscover your passions, and align your life with what truly matters to you. Embrace this sacred journey of self-discovery, for it holds the key to unlocking your fullest potential and living a life of purpose and fulfilment.

Guidance for the Journey

- ❖ **Embrace Authenticity**: The audit is a canvas to discover your true self. Approach it with honesty and vulnerability. Every answer you provide contributes to your unique narrative.
- ❖ **Reflect and Pause:** This is your sanctuary for introspection. Take your time to reflect on each question, allowing the thoughts and emotions to unfold at their own pace.

- ❖ **Celebrate Your Evolution:** As you journey through the audit, you'll unveil your strengths and areas of growth. Acknowledge how far you've come and the untapped potential you hold.
- ❖ **Set Your Intent:** Before you start, set an intention for this process. Is it clarity, transformation, or a renewed sense of purpose? Your intention fuels the depth of your exploration.
- ❖ **Cultivate Patience:** Insight can sometimes surface challenges. Show patience toward yourself as you navigate these moments, knowing that self-awareness is the catalyst for growth.
- ❖ **A Tool for Progress:** Your audit is a dynamic companion. Revisit it periodically, tracking your progress, revising your goals, and celebrating milestones along the way.

Preparing for the Audit

- ❖ **Create Space:** Carve out a calm and uninterrupted environment for your self-reflection. Disconnect from distractions and immerse yourself in the process.
- ❖ **Engage Curiosity:** Approach each question with an inquisitive mind, ready to uncover hidden truths and unveil new perspectives on your life's narrative.
- ❖ **Gather Resources:** Keep a journal, notebook, or digital document for your responses. This not only keeps your thoughts organized but also serves as a record of your journey.
- ❖ **Mindfulness:** As you read each question, take a few deep breaths before responding. Bring your awareness to the task at hand, the room you're in, the emotional state triggered by the prompts. This simple practice enhances focus and invites clarity.
- ❖ **Non-Judgmental Exploration:** Remember, there are no right or wrong answers. Your responses reflect your unique journey and perspective.

As you uncover insights and revelations, consider how they can influence your life's narrative, guiding you towards a future rich with purpose and authenticity. This is your voyage – an expedition towards self-discovery and transformation. The answers you unearth will illuminate your path, helping you embrace your potential and sculpt a life that resonates with your heart's deepest desires.

Personal Audit Prompts

Choose the questions that feel most relevant to your current situation and future aspirations. While we recommend answering at least 5 or 6 questions in each section, feel free to explore and respond to as many as you'd like, as this will provide you with a deeper and more comprehensive self-audit. Remember, not all questions may resonate with you, and that's perfectly fine. Your reflections and insights will serve as valuable resources as you progress through the later stages of the 15-year plan.

Values And Purpose:

These questions invites you to explore your core values and the purpose that fuels your actions. Aligning your choices and pursuits with your values, allow you to cultivate authenticity, fulfilment, and a sense of direction. It prompts you to reflect on the impact your values and purpose have on your decision-making and overall satisfaction in life.

1. Reflect on the earliest memories and experiences that have shaped the core guiding your actions. How have these values evolved over time?
2. How would you describe the fundamental, unchanging convictions that shape your perception of the world and your role in it?
3. Can you pinpoint any specific experiences or people that played a significant role in guiding your life journey?
4. Can you identify key life events that clarified your sense of meaning and purpose in life? What were you doing, and how did it make you feel?
5. How does your sense of purpose contribute to your motivation and focus?
6. Can you recall instances when your values influenced significant decisions?
7. How well do your current actions align with your core values?
8. How do you see your values guiding your future choices and actions?

9. Can you recall instances when external influences tested your core values, and how did you respond to these challenges?

Environment:

Through examining your environment, you gain insight into the forces that either uplift or hinder your progress. Here we invite you to assess your surroundings and make intentional choices to create a supportive and inspiring space that propels you towards your goals.

1. How does your current environment influence your mindset and actions?
2. How have certain environments in your youth played pivotal roles in your development?
3. How do your surroundings impact your overall well-being and productivity?
4. What environments lie on the edge of your comfort zone, and what would it take to get there physically or mentally?
5. Are there individuals in your environment who inspire or motivate you?
6. Reflect on your relationships with individuals who may have held you back or negatively influenced you. How did you handle these situations, and what have you learned from such experiences?
7. Are there changes you can make to create a more supportive and motivating environment?
8. How can you contribute positively to the environment of those around you?
9. Do specific locations or spaces enhance your creativity or focus?
10. How can you actively curate your surroundings to align with your goals and aspirations?

Relationships And Connections:

This part emphasizes the importance of nurturing supportive relationships in your journey. It prompts you to reflect on the quality of your personal and professional connections, communication skills, and collaboration abilities. Evaluating your relationships, can foster a stronger network of individuals who inspire and empower you to reach new heights.

1. Take a moment to assess the quality of your current relationships, both personal and professional. What are the key characteristics of your most valuable connections, and how do they impact your journey?
2. Reflect on the mentors and guides in your life. How have they influenced your path?
3. Can you recall instances where your values played a crucial role in shaping the nature of your connections?
4. Have your early interactions with family, school and your wider eco system, influenced the way you form relationships?
5. Identify the support systems you've built. How do they keep you grounded and motivated?
6. How do you ensure that your connections align with your aspirations and enhance your journey?
7. How do you approach networking to drive your journey forward?
8. Reflect on your role in the lives of those around you. How do you influence and inspire others?
9. What steps can you take to ensure the relationships in your life remain meaningful and continue to fuel your aspirations?

Limiting Beliefs

Explore the power of your beliefs and how they shape your journey. This section delves into the beliefs that might be holding you back, preventing you from reaching your full potential. Recognizing and addressing these limiting beliefs, can unlock new possibilities for personal and professional growth.

These prompts will help you examine your mindset and open the door to positive change on your 15-year journey.

1. Explore your beliefs and thought patterns that may make you hesitant to seek help or guidance from others. How have these beliefs influenced your actions and decisions?
2. Are there limiting beliefs tied to specific past failures or disappointments that continue to affect your confidence?
3. When you think about your core beliefs, do you notice any persistent negative thoughts or self-sabotaging patterns that tend to arise? If so, what are they?
4. Do you fear the potential consequences of success or failure?
5. Are there areas where you've resisted change or expansion due to fear or self-doubt?
6. What do you believe is the highest level of happiness you can achieve in your life, and why?
7. Can you recall instances when you've pushed past your perceived limits and experienced a surge in happiness or personal fulfilment?
8. How can you transform the self-sabotaging thoughts tied to your core beliefs into more positive and empowering thoughts or patterns?
9. What steps can you take to challenge and reframe your limiting beliefs, allowing you to reach a higher level of happiness?

Financial Situation:

This section delves into how your financial choices and mindset influence your overall well-being. Reflecting on your financial situation, provides clarity on your spending habits, financial goals, and values. It prompts you to develop a healthy and empowering relationship with money, allowing you to make sound financial decisions aligned with your aspirations.

1. Can you pinpoint early experiences that shaped your financial beliefs and behaviours?

2. Are you content with your current financial resources, or do you aspire for more?
3. Are there any unhealthy spending habits you would like to address?
4. How open are you to recognizing and seizing opportunities that come your way, whether they relate to career, personal growth, or financial gain?
5. Are there opportunities in your life that you've hesitated to pursue due to fear, self-doubt, or uncertainty? What holds you back from embracing them?
6. How do you view your current financial situation in relation to your well-being?
7. How do you approach financial challenges or setbacks?
8. In what ways can you improve your financial literacy and decision-making?
9. Are there specific financial goals you are actively working towards?
10. How can you balance immediate financial desires with long-term stability?

Capacity (Ability, Learning, Resilience):

Capacity refers to your abilities, skills, and resilience. This part encourages you to assess your strengths and weaknesses, identify areas for improvement, and leverage your unique talents. By cultivating your capacity for learning, adaptability, and resilience, you empower yourself to push beyond your limits and achieve extraordinary results.

1. What are the moments in your life when you felt like you were operating at your absolute best?
2. How would you describe your current abilities, and how have they evolved over time?
3. Can you identify reoccurring moments that weaknesses that have influenced your journey?
4. Think about a time when curiosity led you to acquire new talents or skills, contributing to your capacity. What was the outcome?

5. How do you leverage your unique talents and strengths to achieve exceptional results?
6. Are there times when you surprised yourself with your resilience or creativity during challenging situations?
7. How do you balance pushing your limits with self-care and well-being?
8. What's something you could learn right now, that would make a big difference in what you can achieve?
9. How do you foster a mindset of continuous improvement?

Growth:

These questions invite you to explore your mindset towards growth and learning. It delves into your willingness to step outside your comfort zone, embrace new experiences, and actively seek personal development. Reflect on your growth journey, to unlock the potential to evolve, adapt, and thrive in an ever-changing world.

1. How open are you to learning and embracing new experiences for personal growth?
2. Can you recall instances when stepping out of your comfort zone led to substantial development?
3. How do you approach feedback and use it in your ongoing self-improvement journey?
4. How do you feel about making mistakes and failing? Do you see them as opportunities for growth?
5. Consider how you stay motivated to learn and grow, even during challenging times. What inspires you to persist in your personal development?
6. Are there skills or areas of knowledge you're particularly motivated to develop?
7. Reflect on your past accomplishments. What role did your commitment to continuous learning and growth play in your success?

8. How can you create an environment that supports continuous learning and development?

Consistency/Discipline:

Consistency and discipline are the driving forces behind personal growth and achievement. This section delves into your habits, routines, and level of commitment to your goals. Through frequently evaluating your consistency and discipline, you gain a deeper understanding of how these qualities impact your ability to stay focused, overcome challenges, and achieve lasting success.

1. How consistent are your habits and routines in contributing to your success and personal growth?
2. What are some key factors that contributed to your success during periods of high consistency and discipline?
3. Can you identify areas where you struggle to maintain consistency or discipline?
4. How do you handle challenges that threaten your consistency and discipline?
5. Reflecting on a situation where discipline was pivotal in overcoming a major obstacle or achieving a significant goal. How did you achieve success, and what did you learn?
6. What motivates you to rekindle your consistency and discipline, especially if you've experienced a decline?
7. What strategies do you employ to overcome procrastination and distractions?
8. How do you balance consistency with flexibility and adaptation?
9. How do you sustain consistency when pursuing long-term goals?

Career Reflection:

This section provides an opportunity to reflect on your career journey, accomplishments, and aspirations. It prompts you to assess the alignment between your current career choices and your long-term goals. By examining your career path, you gain clarity on areas for growth, development, and potential career transitions that align with your passions and ambitions.

1. What milestones and experiences have shaped your career journey thus far?
2. Reflecting on your career journey, when have you felt most fulfilled, like you were fulfilling your life's purpose, and why?
3. Are you seeking opportunities for growth and advancement in your field?
4. How have your career goals evolved and shifted from your early professional years to the present, and what influenced these changes?
5. How do you manage challenges in your career path?
6. Can you recall instances where your skills were instrumental in achieving success?
7. How do you ensure your skills continue to evolve in a changing landscape?
8. What are your long-term career aspirations, and how do they relate to your values?
9. How do you define success beyond financial achievements in your career?
10. Are there new areas of expertise you'd like to develop for career enrichment?

Work-Life Balance:

Here we focus on the delicate balance between work and personal life. It invites you to assess how you allocate your time, energy, and attention. Considering your work-life balance, can identify areas for improvement, set boundaries, and prioritize self-care, personal relationships, and activities that bring joy and fulfilment.

1. How well do you balance professional commitments with personal well-being?

2. Can you identify times when work has overshadowed personal commitments?
3. How do you recharge and care for yourself amidst a busy schedule?
4. Are there boundaries you need to establish for a healthier balance?
5. How do you manage burnout or overwhelm related to work-life balance?
6. Consider the times when you were able to achieve more with less effort. How can you apply these insights to improve your work-life balance?
7. Can you pinpoint areas where your work-life balance is particularly effective or challenging, and what lessons can be drawn from these areas?
8. How do you communicate boundaries to colleagues and loved ones?
9. How can you enhance your integration of work and personal life?

Strategic Planning:

It invites you to clarify your long-term vision, break it down into actionable steps, and identify the resources and strategies required for execution. Engaging in strategic planning, can provide you with a detailed roadmap that keeps you focused, motivated, and adaptable in achieving your aspirations.

1. What is your long-term vision for your personal and professional life?
2. What key milestones or accomplishments form the pillars of your journey towards your vision?
3. How do your values and core beliefs infuse your long-term plans with meaning and significance?
4. Are you open to adapting plans as circumstances evolve?
5. How do you incorporate feedback and input from others?
6. How do you measure progress and success in your strategic initiatives?
7. What steps can you take to ensure plans are both ambitious and achievable?

8. How can you maintain motivation and momentum throughout your plans?
9. Imagine sharing your success story with someone you deeply care about. What impact do you want your journey to have on them?

Impact And Legacy:

Here we invite you to contemplate the impact you want to make in the world and the legacy you wish to leave behind. It encourages you to think beyond yourself and consider how your actions can contribute to a greater purpose. It prompts you to align your actions with your values and make choices that create a positive ripple effect in the lives of others. You can leave a lasting imprint and inspire future generations to strive for greatness, by understanding what type of impact and legacy you wish to have.

1. What dreams did you have as a child or young adult that still resonate with you today?
2. If you could give advice to your younger self, what would it be?
3. Reflecting on your life's experiences, what wisdom have you gained that you wish you knew earlier?
4. In what ways have you evolved or changed significantly over the years?
5. Are there any dreams or goals you haven't pursued yet?
6. Can you remember a moment when you positively influenced someone's life? How did that experience shape your understanding of your personal impact?
7. When you look into the future, what are the pillars you would want to define your life story?
8. What stories do you want to reflect your character?
9. What innovative ideas or projects would you like to be associated with in your professional legacy?
10. How can you use your skills, knowledge, and experiences to contribute something lasting?

11. What personal qualities or achievements do you hope will be remembered by your close friends and family?

Through conducting your personal audit, you've likely discovered various aspects of yourself that were previously concealed beneath the surface. As you now find yourself standing on this new ground zero, it's crucial to seize this moment and assimilate all the newfound information about yourself. This process doesn't signify the culmination of your journey; instead, it is only the beginning of the road ahead.

With the illumination gained from your personal audit, you have a clearer understanding of your strengths, weaknesses, passions, and goals. Embrace this newfound awareness and use it as a powerful tool to shape your future path. It's an ongoing journey of self-discovery and growth, where you can continuously fine-tune your course and make necessary adjustments as you progress.

The journey ahead may present challenges and uncertainties, but armed with the insights from your personal audit, you are better equipped to make informed decisions, set meaningful goals, and cultivate a life that aligns with your true self.

Identifying Skills

Now that you have gained an understanding of what underlying factors influence your daily decision, and the direction you truly seek to go in, we will now deep dive into the skills you excel in or are lacking.

By identifying the broad skill categories that align with your desired career path or personal aspirations, you can establish a robust foundation for evaluating your capabilities across various domains. Embrace this opportunity to explore and delve into your skills and capabilities, as it sets the stage for personal growth and empowers you to shape the life you envision.

Remember, this process is not about comparing yourself to others, but rather about understanding and optimizing your individual skill set to reach your fullest potential. Embrace this opportunity wholeheartedly, and with a growth mindset, for it will pave the way for continuous improvement and success as you journey towards your aspirations.

Identifying Skill Categories: Start by identifying broad skill categories that align with your desired career path or personal aspirations. These categories act as base to your skillset and will help you evaluate your capabilities across various domains. Embrace this opportunity to explore your skills and competencies, laying the groundwork for personal growth and the realization of your vision.

Break Down Each Skill Category: Once you have identified the skill categories, break them down further into specific skills or competencies. For example, within the category of communication skills, you can include sub-skills such as public speaking, writing, active listening, and negotiation. This breakdown allows you to assess your proficiency in more granular detail.

Self-Assessment: Evaluate your current proficiency level for each skill within the identified categories. This self-assessment provides an initial snapshot of your skillset and helps you identify areas where improvement is needed.

Prioritize Skills: Consider the relevance of each skill to your desired career path, personal interests, and areas where you want to make an impact. This step helps you focus your efforts on the skills that will have the greatest impact on your success.

Identify Skill Gaps: Compare your self-assessment ratings with the prioritized skills. Identify the gaps between your current skill levels and the desired proficiency for each skill. These skill gaps represent the areas where you need to concentrate your learning and development efforts. Recognizing these gaps helps you allocate resources effectively and address areas of weakness.

Set Learning Objectives: Establish clear learning objectives for each prioritized skill. Define what you want to achieve and the level of proficiency you aim to reach within each skill. Setting clear objectives helps guide your learning journey and provides a benchmark for tracking your progress.

Create A Learning Plan: Develop a learning plan that outlines the actions and steps you will take to acquire and enhance the prioritized skills. Consider various learning methods and resources, such as courses, workshops, online tutorials, mentorship, practice opportunities, and experiential learning. Determine the resources, tools, and support you will need to facilitate your learning journey. This plan provides a roadmap for skill development and helps you stay organized and focused.

Implement And Track Progress: Take action on your learning plan and actively engage in acquiring and developing the identified skills. Regularly track your progress by monitoring your skill development, seeking feedback from others, and reflecting on your growth.

Evaluate And Update: Periodically reassess your skill levels and evaluate your progress against your learning objectives. Reflect on how the acquired skills have contributed to your personal and professional growth. Identify new skills that may become relevant and update your skills audit accordingly.

By following these steps in the Skills Audit framework, you can conduct a thorough assessment of your skills, create a targeted learning plan, and continuously develop the competencies necessary for your long-term success. Regular evaluation and updates ensure that your skills remain relevant and aligned with your evolving goals over the next 15 years.

Bench Marking

When conducting a personal audit and assessing personal skills, it can be valuable to use benchmarks as reference points to gauge your proficiency and progress. Here are two key benchmarks to consider:

Comparative Analysis: Compare your skills to those of peers or professionals in similar roles or industries. This can be achieved through networking, participating in industry forums or events, or researching case studies and success stories of individuals who have excelled in the area you are assessing. Observing the skills and achievements of others, can provide insights into the expected standards and identify areas where you may need improvement.

Comparison to Industry Standards: Research industry standards or best practices related to the specific skill you are assessing. Explore resources such as professional associations, certifications, or job descriptions that outline the expected skill level or competency for a given role or field. These industry standards serve as benchmarks to understand what is considered proficient or exemplary within the industry. Aligning your skills with industry expectations, can better highlight your strengths and areas for growth.

It's essential to approach benchmarking with a positive mindset, understanding that it is not about comparing yourself to others in a negative or competitive way. Instead, it is a tool to provide a reference point and help you understand where you currently stand in relation to your goals. Benchmarking can motivate you to improve and set realistic targets for personal growth and development.

Remember that everyone's journey is unique, and progress should be measured against your own goals and aspirations. Use benchmarks as a source of inspiration and guidance, adapting them to your individual circumstances and desired outcomes. By leveraging benchmarks effectively, you can gain valuable insights, set meaningful goals, and chart a path towards continuous improvement

Skills Assessment Rating System

Embarking on the path of self-discovery through skill assessment is a transformative journey. As you navigate each skill category, you'll uncover your strengths, identify areas for growth, and map out your development strategy. Use the self-assessment rating system below to honestly evaluate your current proficiency level in each skill:

N: Novice - I possess minimal to no experience or understanding of this skill.

B: Beginner - I hold a fundamental understanding but require substantial guidance and practice.

I: Intermediate - I possess a moderate proficiency level, adept at handling tasks with occasional challenges.

A: Advanced - I am skilled and confident, capable of managing intricate tasks with ease.

E: Expert - I am highly proficient, confidently navigating advanced challenges and even guiding others.

For each skill category, circle the letter that best aligns with your current competency. Embrace this self-assessment as a powerful tool for growth, enabling you to refine your skills and unlock your full potential.

Skill Categories

1. Personal and Professional Development:

- ❖ Self-awareness (N B I A E)
- ❖ Emotional intelligence (N B I A E)
- ❖ Self-motivation (N B I A E)
- ❖ Adaptability (N B I A E)
- ❖ Resilience (N B I A E)
- ❖ Growth mindset (N B I A E)
- ❖ Continuous learning (N B I A E)
- ❖ Goal setting and accountability (N B I A E)

2. Organizational Efficiency:

- ❖ Time management (N B I A E)
- ❖ Prioritization (N B I A E)

- ❖ Planning and scheduling (N B I A E)
- ❖ Multitasking (N B I A E)
- ❖ Resource management (N B I A E)
- ❖ Task delegation (N B I A E)
- ❖ Attention to detail (N B I A E)

3. Analytical and Critical Thinking:

- ❖ Critical thinking (N B I A E)
- ❖ Data analysis and interpretation (N B I A E)
- ❖ Statistical analysis (N B I A E)
- ❖ Problem-solving (N B I A E)
- ❖ Logical reasoning (N B I A E)
- ❖ Systems thinking (N B I A E)
- ❖ Quantitative skills (N B I A E)

4. Technical and Industry-Specific Skills:

- ❖ Programming and coding (N B I A E)
- ❖ Graphic design (N B I A E)
- ❖ Digital marketing (N B I A E)
- ❖ Web development (N B I A E)
- ❖ Software proficiency (e.g., Adobe Creative Suite) (N B I A E)
- ❖ Trend Forecasting (N B I A E)
- ❖ Product knowledge (N B I A E)
- ❖ Research and development (N B I A E)

5. Communication and Leadership:

- ❖ Written communication (N B I A E)
- ❖ Verbal communication (N B I A E)
- ❖ Presentation skills (N B I A E)
- ❖ Public speaking (N B I A E)
- ❖ Negotiation and persuasion (N B I A E)
- ❖ Team leadership (N B I A E)
- ❖ Conflict resolution (N B I A E)

❖ Coaching and mentoring (N B I A E)

6. Creative and Innovative Thinking:

❖ Idea generation and brainstorming (N B I A E)
❖ Visual expression and creativity (N B I A E)
❖ Content creation (N B I A E)
❖ Design and aesthetics (N B I A E)
❖ Innovation and design thinking (N B I A E)
❖ Creative problem-solving (N B I A E)

7. Financial Management and Analysis:

❖ Budgeting and financial planning (N B I A E)
❖ Investment strategies (N B I A E)
❖ Financial reporting and analysis (N B I A E)
❖ Tax planning and compliance (N B I A E)
❖ Financial risk management (N B I A E)
❖ Cash flow management (N B I A E)
❖ Corporate finance (N B I A E)

8. Interpersonal and Collaborative Skills:

❖ Active listening (N B I A E)
❖ Interpersonal skills (N B I A E)
❖ Cross-cultural communication (N B I A E)
❖ Relationship building (N B I A E)
❖ Team collaboration (N B I A E)
❖ Networking (N B I A E)
❖ Customer service (N B I A E)

Pro Tip: Transferable Skills

Transferable skills, often referred to as "soft skills," are a critical component of career success. These skills can be applied across various industries and job roles and are essential for individuals looking to expand their knowledge and adapt to new situations and challenges. Unlike technical skills, which are specific to a particular job or industry, transferable skills are skills that can be transferred from one area of life to another.

The ability to learn new skills quickly and to apply them effectively in different contexts is essential in today's fast-paced and rapidly changing world. Once individuals have identified their transferable skills, they can leverage them to advance their careers by highlighting them on their resumes and in job interviews. For instance, an individual who has worked as a project manager may have developed skills in leadership, communication, and problem-solving that could be applied to other roles in management or consulting. They can also seek out opportunities to develop and apply these skills in different contexts, such as by taking on new projects or volunteering for leadership roles in professional organizations.

Developing transferable skills involves taking steps such as developing adjacent skills to one's industry, completing courses outside of one's field of work, attending professional development workshops, and understanding core principles that are universal regardless of industry. Once an individual has a clear long-term vision for their life, they can work backward, plotting the different areas they will need to develop skills for and the existing skills they have that can start to build upon.

Transferable skills are vital for career success in today's fast-paced and rapidly changing world. By developing and leveraging these skills, individuals can adapt to new situations and challenges and bring valuable knowledge and experience to different roles and organizations. With the advent of technology, online resources, and communities, individuals have more options than ever before to develop and improve their transferable skills.

Chapter Summary

Congratulations on having the courage to delve into the depths of your mind and audit your life. The deep work you have undertaken through the chapter has provided you with a solid foundation for a better and more purposeful life than you could have ever imagined.

Through deep introspection and self-reflection, you audited various aspects of your life, unearthing valuable insights into your subconscious and the skills you have developed along the way. By reflecting on the various segments that create your life, you have gained a profound understanding of how the various factors ultimately shaped your personality, beliefs, and mindset. This process has provided you with a clear understanding of where you currently stand and has revealed both areas of alignment and opportunities for improvement.

Assessing your strengths and weaknesses played a crucial role in this chapter, enabling you to leverage your skills effectively and identify areas for growth. You evaluated your capacity to learn, cope with stress, and prioritize your physical and mental well-being. The Personal Audit prompts you to uncover and confront limiting beliefs that may be holding you back. Recognizing these barriers is the first step toward breaking free from them. We took strides toward a more stable future through financial introspection, examining your relationship with money and developing a clear understanding of your current situation, goals, and management practices.

Above all, the Personal Audit guided you to explore the values and purpose that give your life meaning. It's about looking inward and recognizing factors that influence who we are, that may have been hiding beneath the surface. Armed with this newfound understanding, you now possess the tools to align your actions with your purpose, setting the stage for positive impact and a legacy worth leaving behind. As you move forward, let these insights be the North Star guiding you on your continuous journey of personal and professional growth.

CHAPTER 2: DEFINING YOUR VISION

Determining Your Vision

Aclear vision goes beyond short-term goals; it is placed on our horizon and encompasses a larger picture and timespan for becoming who you aspire to be. When you gain clarity about your future self and articulate your vision for the next 15 years, setting goals and mapping out the path to achieve them becomes remarkably straightforward. Your vision becomes the anchor that keeps you focused, motivated, and aligned with your purpose.

It is essential to understand that your vision is unique to you. It should reflect your deepest desires, aspirations, and values. It goes beyond superficial goals and taps into the core of who you are and what you want to achieve. Whether it is financial freedom, personal fulfilment, a thriving career, or a harmonious lifestyle, your vision should encompass the full spectrum of your dreams.

Through defining your vision, you gain clarity about what you want to accomplish, who you want to become, and why it truly matters to you. This clarity acts as a compass, orienting you towards your long-term goals and providing a sense of direction amidst the challenges and distractions along the way. Throughout this chapter, be specific and deliberate in your vision to lay the groundwork for a clear roadmap that will lead you towards your desired destination.

Step 1: Identify What Matters Most

The first step in defining your vision is to reflect on your core values and passions. This involves taking the time to identify what truly matters to you, what brings you the most joy and fulfilment, and what motivates you to pursue your goals. These answers would have come to light during your personal audit. Reflecting on your values will help you to identify what is truly important to you and what you want to prioritize in your life over this journey.

Next, consider your interests and hobbies. What are the things that you enjoy doing in your free time? What activities bring you the most pleasure and fulfilment? By identifying your passions, you can begin to think about how you can incorporate them into your long-term goals and vision.

Finally, think about the things that ignite your enthusiasm and inspire you. This could be a cause or issue that you are passionate about, a particular career path, or a goal that you have always wanted to achieve. Self-reflection is the best way to see your true self, so by reflecting on what inspires you will help you to create a vision that is meaningful and fulfilling, and that motivates you to take action towards achieving your goals.

Step 2: Envision Your Ideal Future

Once you have reflected on your core values and passions, the next step in defining your vision is to envision your ideal future. This involves using your imagination to paint a vivid picture of what you want your life to look like in various aspects, including career, relationships, health, personal development, and contributions to society. Your vision will evolve with you as you progress through your phases, so give yourself the needed space and be flexible with these changes.

Career And Professional Life

Visualize Your Dream Career Or Professional Life: Imagine yourself 15 years from now, engaged in a fulfilling and rewarding job or entrepreneurial venture that aligns with your passions and values. Picture the specific role, industry, or business you want to be a part of, and envision the impact you want to make.

Identify Your Key Objectives And Milestones: Define the specific goals and milestones you want to achieve in your career. Consider factors such as promotions, industry recognition, or business growth. Outline the components of each milestone and the skills or knowledge you need to acquire along the way.

Relationships

Imagine Your Ideal Relationships: Envision the quality and depth of your relationships with family, friends, and significant others. Picture the types of connections that bring you joy, support, and a sense of belonging. Visualize the specific activities or experiences you want to share with your loved ones.

Define Your Values And Priorities: Reflect on the values and priorities you want to prioritize in your relationships. Consider aspects such as trust, communication, shared values, and emotional support. Determine the actions and behaviours that align with these values and will contribute to the growth and strength of your relationships.

Health And Well-being

Envision Optimal Physical And Mental Health: Visualize yourself in a state of optimal well-being, both physically and mentally. Imagine engaging in regular exercise, maintaining a nutritious diet, and practicing self-care routines. Picture yourself full of vitality and energy, able to pursue your goals and passions with vigour.

Set Health And Well-Being Goals: Define specific health and well-being goals that you want to achieve across your journey. This could include targets such as weight management, fitness levels, stress reduction, or mental resilience. Outline the habits you need to adopt to attain and maintain these goals.

Personal Development And Growth

Visualize Continuous Learning And Growth: Envision yourself continuously learning, acquiring new skills, and expanding your knowledge and expertise. Picture yourself engaging in personal growth activities such as reading, attending workshops, or pursuing further education. Imagine the person you want to become and the steps you need to take to reach that level of personal development.

Identify Areas Of Personal Growth: Reflect on the areas of personal growth and development that are important to you. This could include professional skills, emotional intelligence, leadership abilities, or creativity. Set specific goals for each area and outline the actions and resources required to enhance your personal growth.

Contributions To Society

Envision Your Impact And Contributions: Visualize the positive difference you want to make in society and the world around you. Imagine how you can contribute to causes that align with your values, whether through volunteering, advocacy, philanthropy, or any other means. Picture yourself actively involved in making a meaningful impact.

Identify Your Areas Of Contribution: Define the specific causes or areas where you want to focus your contributions. This could include environmental sustainability, social justice, education, or community development. Determine the actions and resources you can dedicate towards these causes and outline measurable objectives for your contributions.

By vividly envisioning your ideal future in these various aspects, you will gain clarity on what success and fulfilment mean to you personally and professionally. This vision will serve as a compass, guiding your actions and decisions over the next 15 years. It will inspire and motivate you to align your goals and actions with the vision you have created, enabling you to build the life you truly desire. Remember to dream big and let your imagination lead the way as you articulate and pursue your goals within the plan.

Step 3: Set Bold And Inspiring Goals

Transitioning from envisioning your ideal future to turning it into reality requires turning your vision into tangible and actionable goals. This pivotal step empowers you to bridge the gap between dreams and achievements. As you embark on this journey of goal setting, it is important to recognize that your starting point does not define your ultimate capacity. Instead, aim to set goals that reflect the potential of the person you are striving to become.

Connect With Personal Values And Passions: Ensure your goals are inspiring and meaningful to you personally. Link them to your core values and passions, as this connection generates motivation and commitment. When your goals align with your values and excite you, they become powerful drivers of action.

Strike A Balance Between Ambition And Achievability: Aim for goals that challenge you to grow and push your abilities, while remaining realistic and achievable with your current resources and skills. These goals can scale up with you over time.

Make Your Goals Specific And Measurable: Avoid setting vague goals by defining concrete objectives. Instead of saying "improve my career," set a specific goal like "earn a promotion to a leadership position within my field within five years" or "start my own business within 10 years." Specific goals provide clarity and measurable criteria to assess progress.

Incorporate An Element Of Stretch: Force yourself beyond your comfort zone and challenge your perceived limitations. Seek to achieve goals that require you to develop new skills, expand your knowledge, or take calculated risks. Consider your current skills, resources, and timeframe to determine the level of stretch that is realistic for you.

Consider Broader Impact: Evaluate how your goals contribute to the betterment of not just your own life, but also the lives of others or society as a whole. When your goals have a sense of purpose and contribute to a greater cause, they become even more inspiring and meaningful.

Document your goals and keep them visible as a constant reminder of what you are working towards. Regularly review and reassess your goals, making adjustments as necessary based on changing circumstances, interests, or priorities. These goals serve as guideposts, directing your actions and choices as you strive to transform your vision into reality.

Step 4: Prioritize And Focus

After setting bold and inspiring goals, it is crucial to prioritize and focus on the goals that align with your overall vision. Begin by evaluating each goal in relation to your vision and values. Reflect on their significance and potential impact on your life. Identify the goals that resonate most strongly with your vision and have the potential to make a significant positive difference.

As you prioritize your goals, consider the concept of momentum building. Rather than pursuing an excessive number of goals simultaneously, focus on selecting a few key goals that, when achieved, will create a domino effect of success. Choose carefully and intentionally, time is your biggest currency so selecting goals that complement and reinforce each other, can create a synergy that propels you forward. This intentional alignment allows for a cumulative impact, where each accomplishment builds upon the previous one, creating a snowball effect of progress.

To avoid spreading yourself too thin, consider the resources, time, and energy required for each goal, be mindful of any conflicts or overlaps between goals. Evaluate if you have the necessary resources or need to allocate them appropriately. Maintaining focus on your prioritized goals is essential. Regularly review and reassess your goals and priorities as circumstances change. Stay flexible and adjust your goals to remain aligned with your evolving vision.

Embracing Bucket List Goals

We often find ourselves caught up in the hustle and bustle of daily life, chasing success, and fulfilling responsibilities. Life is not merely about the passage of time; it's about making the moments count. Amidst all the busyness, it is essential to pause and consider what truly brings meaning to our lives: creating memories with those who matter and pursuing our bucket list goals.

A bucket list is more than just a list of wishes; it's a testament to our desires, dreams, and passions. It represents the experiences we long to have, the places we wish to explore, and the adventures we yearn to embark upon.

Infuse your life with flavour and excitement, to make this journey into the future something worth living for.

Imagine standing atop a mountain peak, feeling the exhilaration of conquering a fear of heights; seeing clouds roll across the ground below. Picture yourself exploring vibrant cultures and indulging in unique cuisines during your travels around the world. These breath-taking moments are part of the life blood of human existence.

Each year becomes an opportunity to tick off items from our list, creating memories that will be etched in our hearts forever. Whether big or small, every experience adds depth and richness to our lives, making the journey more meaningful and rewarding. Life is meant to be lived; we cannot forget the fact that the planet we live on is filled with so many opportunities to expand our horizons. Including bucket list goals in your 15-Year Plan is an intentional steps towards a deeper feeling of fulfilment in your life.

Yet, amidst the pursuit of personal dreams, it is vital to remember that life's true essence lies in the relationships we cultivate. Family, friends, and loved ones are the threads that weave together the fabric of our lives. They are the ones who share in our joys, support us during challenging times, and make our successes more meaningful. It's about strengthening bonds and creating lasting memories with those who matter most. Incorporating meaningful moments into your journey allows us to nurture these relationships intentionally. It's about creating space for quality time with loved ones, sharing laughter, tears, and cherished moments.

Look to create a harmonious balance between personal growth and shared experiences. The journey becomes more fulfilling when we have our loved ones by our side, cheering us on and celebrating our victories. These moments of togetherness become the heartwarming memories that shape the tapestry of our lives and are exactly what we look back on fondly during our later years.

Your roadmap shouldn't be filled with only professional success or individual achievements; there will be many milestones outside of this realm that will serve as some of your core memories. It is about embracing a rounded approach to life, infusing our days with goals and cherishing relationships, to create a journey of fulfilment, purpose, and joy, which is not linked to only our career achievements.

As we embark on this 15-year journey, let us remember that life's true treasures lay beyond our net worth. By daring to dream, exploring the world, and sharing experiences with those who matter, we can infuse our lives with a profound sense of fulfilment.

Pro Tip: The Decision-Making Framework

In every facet of life, we encounter a multitude of decisions that shape our present and influence our future. From everyday choices to pivotal crossroads, our ability to make sound decisions is a fundamental skill that profoundly impacts our personal growth, relationships, and professional success. However, decision-making can be a complex process, fraught with emotions, biases, and the abundance of available information.

To navigate this intricate landscape with confidence and clarity, we must embrace the power of an enhanced and flexible decision-making framework. Such a framework empowers us to methodically approach choices, ensuring we consider all pertinent factors, evaluate options thoroughly, and make well-informed and impactful decisions.

In this seven-step decision-making framework, we will explore a systematic and adaptable process supported by various techniques and considerations. With these steps, you will be better equipped to tackle decisions of any magnitude, from career moves to financial investments or even day-to-day choices. Let's delve into the components of this framework and arm ourselves with the tools to make informed choices that align with our goals and values.

Step 1 - Identify the Decision: To begin, take the time to clearly define the decision you need to make. Understand the context, background, and any constraints that might influence the decision. Delve deep into the core intent or purpose behind this decision and recognize the broader implications it could have on various aspects of your life. Be mindful of emotional biases that may cloud your judgment and strive for objectivity by considering all relevant information.

Step 2 - Gather Relevant Information: In this step, collect all pertinent information related to the decision at hand. Utilize various sources, such as qualitative research, reports, analytics, expert opinions, and feedback from others. Ensure you have a comprehensive understanding of the potential risks, opportunities, and consequences associated with each option. Dive into the nuances, patterns , and intricacies of the available information, and actively listen to diverse perspectives to gain deeper insights.

Step 3 - Define Decision Criteria: Establishing a clear criterion for decisions is crucial for making objective evaluations. Define the specific factors that will guide your judgment in weighing the options. Rank these criteria based on their importance and relevance to your situation. These could be factors such as cost-effectiveness, feasibility, ethical considerations, long-term impact, alignment with your core values, stakeholder interests, and environmental and social implications.

Step 4 - Generate Options: Here, we unleash your creativity and explore a wide array of potential options or solutions to the problem. Encourage brainstorming and seek diverse perspectives to generate alternatives. Refrain from prematurely evaluating or dismissing ideas, allowing a free flow of creativity. Consult with others to uncover fresh viewpoints and additional options. Remember, the best decision isn't always the most obvious; it may emerge from a unique combination of instinct and insight.

Step 5 - Evaluate Options: Thoroughly analyse each option against the defined decision criteria. Whenever possible, quantify the potential outcomes to gain a clearer perspective. Consider the short-term and long-term effects of each option on various stakeholders and aspects of your life. Identify the trade-offs and potential risks associated with each alternative, and carefully weigh their pros and cons, including the ethical and environmental impact.

Step 6 - Consider Future Scenarios: Anticipate potential future scenarios and assess how each option might perform under different conditions. This foresight will help you select a more robust and adaptable solution that can withstand various challenges and uncertainties. Align your decision with a vision that reflects your long-term aspirations, not just short-term goals.

Step 7 - Learn and Iterate: After making the decision, evaluate the outcomes and learn from the experience. Embrace a culture of continuous improvement and learning from both successful and unsuccessful decisions. Use the feedback loop to refine the decision-making process and adapt the framework for future decisions.

Remember that decision-making is both an art and a science. It involves a combination of rational analysis, emotional intelligence, creativity, and adaptability. Practice and refine your decision-making skills over time, and be open to seeking feedback from others to continually improve your ability to make effective choices.

Chapter Summary

In this transformative chapter, you've started on a journey to shape the trajectory of your personal odyssey. It's all about crafting a vision that will be your guiding light, illuminating the path to a more fulfilling future. This vision is a blueprint for the life you aspire to lead, and the positive change you aim to bring about.

The chapter emphasizes the art of striking a balance between ambition and attainability, ensuring your goals are specific and measurable. These goals should serve as both challenges and resonances with your values, offering the fuel for long-term success.

It underscores the significance of creating memories and wholeheartedly embracing bucket list goals. Life isn't solely about professional triumphs; it's also about cherishing moments that hold meaning and excitement. The chapter reminds us of the importance of nurturing relationships and achieving equilibrium between personal growth and shared experiences.

We introduced a practical decision-making framework, highlighting the value of making well-informed choices across various facets of life. This seven-step framework provides a methodical approach, considering all relevant factors, and leading to sound decision-making.

As you lay the groundwork for your success, remember that this journey is a dynamic process of growth and self-discovery. The upcoming chapters will equip you with essential tools and strategies to breathe life into your vision.

CHAPTER 3: PHASES

Phases

In the second chapter, we explored the essence of your vision and how it aligns with your core values. This understanding has provided the foundation for your immediate and long-term goals. Now, we need to build this into a complete plan of attack.

In the vast canvas of life, a 15-year plan isn't just a list of dreams; it's your detailed guide to turning aspirations into achievable goals. Within this plan, phases emerge as the pivotal milestones that guide your journey. These phases are the building blocks, the segments of your life's masterpiece that allow your complex vision to unfold gracefully across the canvas of time.

By breaking your journey into phases, you'll discover that your objectives become more attainable. These periods serve as the stepping stones in your plan, transforming the grand vision you have for your life into tangible, manageable segments. It's important to note that the duration of each phase may vary from person to person; what's three years for one might be two for another. This flexibility ensures that your aspirations are not just dreams but concrete goals, each phase providing the brushstrokes to paint the picture of your self-actualization journey over the entire 15-year timeline.

Having distinct stages provide the structure and framework necessary to navigate your journey with clarity, focus, and purpose. Each phase of your plan offers unique opportunities for skill development, knowledge acquisition, and personal transformation. Intentionally allocating time and resources, then setting goals within each phase, continuously build the capabilities and foundation needed to progress towards your long-term goals. Embracing the journey as a series of interconnected phases will allow you to incorporate valuable insights and course corrections from one stage into the next.

While it may be challenging to envision the details of the later phases, especially beyond the first year, it is important to understand that the earlier phases lay the groundwork for future clarity and progression. This sense of direction and purpose prevents you from feeling adrift and ensures that you are always moving towards your ultimate destination.

Having a larger vision beyond the current plan allows you to seamlessly transition to the next phase of growth and development. You may find yourself achieving and surpassing goals earlier than expected!

Grounding The Phases

As you embark on your journey through each phase, take a moment to evaluate whether the goals you've set are truly essential, impulsive desires or bucket list goals. Crafting an exceptional life might entail making sacrifices in certain aspects of your lifestyle for specific durations, ensuring you achieve your coveted outcomes.

It's natural to be drawn to what we want, often overlooking the necessity of what we need during certain stretches. Be prepared for chapters in your life where you must embrace tasks that may not bring immediate joy but are vital for propelling your plans forward. There will be instances when you need to dedicate six months, fully immersing yourself in activities that your goals demand. Consider this; if you were to let your goals slip away at a critical juncture simply because you didn't fully commit when it was necessary, how would that make you feel?

Envisioning lofty aspirations should always have a solid foundation in practical building blocks that render achievement plausible. Take time to reflect on your answers to the personal audit and these additional prompts below, to give you deeper clarity on how your phases should be mapped out.

Value Clarification:

1. How do the goals I've set for this phase align with my overarching life purpose and core values?
2. Are there any adjustments needed to ensure that the outcomes of this phase contribute authentically to my personal and professional growth?
3. How can I weave my passions and values into the actions and decisions I make during this phase?

41

4. What impact will achieving the goals of this phase have on my long-term vision and the legacy I want to create?
5. How can I ensure that my pursuit of these goals aligns with my ethical principles and promotes personal fulfilment?

Leveraging Networks:

1. Who in my professional and personal network can offer valuable insights, mentorship, or collaboration opportunities during this phase?
2. How can I actively engage with my network to generate new ideas, opportunities, and partnerships that align with this phase's goals?
3. What strategies can I employ to expand and diversify my network to access fresh perspectives and resources?
4. How can I give back to my network in ways that align with my values and contribute to mutual growth?
5. How will I maintain a balance between nurturing existing relationships and cultivating new connections to maximize my progress in this phase?

Legacy Building:

1. How do the achievements and outcomes of this phase contribute to the broader legacy I aspire to leave behind?
2. What steps can I take during this phase to ensure that my contributions align with my long-term impact goals?
3. What relationships or partnerships can I cultivate during this phase to extend the reach and endurance of my legacy?
4. How can I infuse purpose and meaning into each action I take, ensuring that they resonate with the legacy I wish to establish?

Adaptation and Resilience:

1. What potential obstacles or disruptions can I anticipate in this phase, and how can I develop contingency plans to address them?
2. How can I cultivate a growth mindset that enables me to learn from setbacks and maintain my resilience in the face of challenges?

3. What strategies can I employ to proactively manage stress and maintain my well-being throughout this phase?
4. How will I ensure that unexpected changes or shifts in circumstances won't derail my progress toward this phase's goals?
5. What practices can I integrate into my routine to foster adaptability and quick thinking, allowing me to pivot effectively when necessary?
6. What strategies can I use to overcome periods of stagnation or setbacks and keep moving forward?

Resource Alignment:

1. How can I allocate my time, finances, and energy effectively to ensure I make substantial progress in this phase?
2. Are there any potential resource gaps that might hinder my success in this phase, and how can I address them proactively?
3. How can I optimize my current skillset and assets to maximize the impact of this phase's goals?
4. What support systems or external resources can I tap into to amplify my efforts during this phase?
5. How can I strike a balance between pushing myself to achieve ambitious goals and maintaining a sustainable pace to prevent burnout?
6. How will I define and quantify success for the goals I've set in this phase, allowing me to assess progress effectively?

As well as mapping out what you want to achieve, these questions will help you understand your resources and how your network can help you achieve your projected goals. Every endeavour comes at a cost. Your financial stability often dictates your quality of life. While allowing your imagination to soar with boundless dreams, anchor your aspirations with good habits, steadfast values, and actionable strategies. This fusion of audacious vision and practical groundwork will empower your ambitions to not only take flight but soar to unprecedented heights.

Make It Measurable And Time-Bound

To truly realize your 15-year aspirations, it's essential to set tangible benchmarks and deadlines. This not only helps you monitor and gauge your progress but also pinpoints areas needing improvement. While a 15-year target may seem overwhelming, dissecting it into smaller, attainable milestones makes it more digestible. By ensuring each goal is quantifiable and set within a specific timeframe, you pave a clear path towards actualizing your overarching life vision.

Start by making your goals measurable. This means defining clear criteria or metrics that will allow you to assess your progress and determine when a goal has been achieved. For instance, if your aspiration is to establish multiple businesses and achieve a turnover of £10 million within the next 15 years, you can make this goal measurable by setting specific targets across your phases I.e., you can aim to launch your first business within the first year. This serves as a concrete milestone that indicates progress towards your overarching objective. Additionally, you can set a target of reaching a certain revenue milestone, such as £1 million, within the first five years.

These measurable targets provide clear checkpoints that enable you to track your progress and make necessary adjustments along the way, ensuring you stay on track towards building a successful and profitable portfolio of businesses. When your goals are measurable, you gain clarity on what success looks like and can monitor your progress effectively. It also helps you stay motivated by providing a sense of achievement and allowing you to celebrate milestones along the way.

Next, make your goals time-bound by setting specific timelines or deadlines. Assigning a timeframe to each goal creates a sense of urgency and helps you stay focused and accountable. Consider the 15-year timeframe as a whole and then break it down into shorter intervals, such as annual, 3-year or 5-year goals.

When setting time-bound goals, be realistic and consider factors such as the complexity of the goal, available resources, and personal circumstances. Avoid setting timelines that are too rigid or unrealistic, as this can lead to unnecessary pressure and disappointment. Instead, aim for a balance between challenge and achievability, allowing yourself enough time to make meaningful progress while maintaining a sense of urgency. Dividing your long-term vision into shorter timeframes, you create a roadmap that guides your progress over the years. Each smaller goal serves as a steppingstone towards the larger vision.

When breaking down your goals, consider the specific actions and milestones that need to be achieved within each timeframe. This allows you to focus on immediate objectives while keeping the bigger picture in mind. Regularly review and reassess your goals, adjusting timelines or milestones as needed to stay aligned with your vision and adapt to changing circumstances.

Framework For Mapping Out Phases

By now you would have been able to define your vision, values, goals, and complete your skills and personal audits. These are no small orders and will have required you to be very transparent and honest with yourself. Now, let's transform these components into a dynamic and adaptable 15-year plan that propels you toward realizing your aspirations. Remember, while this framework provides structure, it's designed to be flexible and align with your unique journey.

Step 1- Integrate Your Vision, Values, And Goals:

The heartbeat of your plan is the seamless weaving of your vision, values, and goals. Each phase should resonate deeply with your overarching life purpose. Your vision is your compass, illuminating the path ahead, while your values serve as the foundation for your decisions. Ensure that the goals you set align harmoniously, are built intentionally and strategically as you progress through the phases.

- ❖ Align phases with your vision and core values by revisiting your vision statement and values regularly.
- ❖ Ensure your goals resonate with your life purpose by reviewing the personal audit and vision crafting prompts, at different stages of your journey.

❖ Let your vision guide decisions at each phase by considering if each decision moves you closer to your vision.

Step 2 - Building Progressive Phases:

Strike a balance between immediate, tangible objectives and the far-reaching scope of your life vision. Visualize how the skills you've identified, and personal values can stack on top of one another within each phase, creating a strong and meaningful narrative.

❖ Construct interconnected steppingstones for progression by breaking down your long-term vision into smaller milestones.
❖ Balance short-term objectives and long-term vision by setting weekly, monthly or quarterly objectives that contribute to your larger goals.
❖ Weave skills and values into each phase's narrative by identifying how your skills and values can be applied to each phase.

Step 3- Skill Development And Continuous Learning:

Your skills are the bedrock of your growth. Designate specific phases for honing and expanding your skillset. Dedicate time to deliberate practice and real-world application, as these periods lay the foundation for your competence. Consider how each phase contributes to the tapestry of skills that will carry you through your journey. Dedicate time in phases to enhancing your skillset by setting aside focused practice sessions.

❖ Dedicate periods of your phases to enhancing your skillset by setting aside focused practice sessions.
❖ Allocate time for practice and real-world application by identifying real-world scenarios where you can apply your skills.
❖ Consider how each phase contributes to skill growth by reflecting on how your skills have evolved in each phase.

Step 4 - Network And Team Building:

A robust network enriches your journey. Craft phases to deliberately expand both your professional and personal connections. Thoughtfully cultivate relationships that align with your aspirations and values. Collaborators and mentors become essential guides, amplifying your growth trajectory through shared insights and diverse perspectives.

- ❖ Build a diverse network by connecting with individuals from various backgrounds and industries.
- ❖ Seek out mentors who can provide guidance and support tailored to your goals.
- ❖ Collaborate with like-minded professionals to leverage collective knowledge and resources.
- ❖ Place yourself in the highest value rooms you can access, or dive within your network to seek out opportunities through mutual connections, enriching your path further.

Step 5 - Financial Planning And Living Standards:

Your financial health is crucial for realizing the dreams and aspirations outlined in your plan. It's about creating a tailored financial roadmap that aligns with each stage of your life's journey. Focus on balancing your current lifestyle needs with your future ambitions. As you move forward, your financial strategy should be flexible, evolving to meet both your immediate requirements and long-term ambitions.

- ❖ Craft a detailed financial plan that caters to both your immediate and future needs, setting clear short-term and long-term financial goals.
- ❖ Make it a habit to routinely assess and fine-tune your financial plan, ensuring it stays relevant to your life's changing situations and goals.
- ❖ Concentrate on saving and investing in ways that resonate with your personal financial targets, ensuring every dollar is a step towards your life's ambitions.

Step 6 - Family And Personal Achievements:

While personal goals are paramount, family dynamics can play a pivotal role. This may involve setting aside a period in the future for endeavours beyond the professional sphere, such as intentionally starting a family or nurturing existing relationships. Set aside time in your phases to celebrate personal milestones and cherish quality time with loved ones. These phases encapsulate the harmony between your individual journey and the shared moments that bring meaning and joy to your life.

- ❖ Dedicate quality time to family and loved ones, nurturing those relationships.
- ❖ Celebrate personal achievements and milestones to maintain a balanced and fulfilling life.
- ❖ Prioritize self-care and well-being to ensure you're at your best for both personal and professional endeavours.

Step 7 - Bucket List Goals:

Infuse your journey with excitement and adventure by dedicating time in your phases to those once-in-a-lifetime experiences. Balance practical goals with audacious dreams, ensuring that your 15-year plan encompasses not only achievement but also unforgettable moments of exploration and self-discovery.

- ❖ Expand networks in both personal and professional spheres by attending networking events and reaching out to potential contacts.
- ❖ Foster relationships aligned with goals and values by identifying common goals and values during conversations.
- ❖ Amplify growth through collaborators and mentors by actively seeking out mentorship and collaboration opportunities.

Step 8 - Legacy And Meaning:

Leave an indelible mark beyond personal achievements. Dedicate phases to projects that contribute to your legacy – whether in your community, industry, or beyond. Consider the lasting impact you want to leave and how your phases can reflect a purpose-driven path that extends far beyond yourself.

- ❖ Dedicate phases to projects beyond personal achievements by identifying meaningful projects that contribute to a larger purpose.
- ❖ Consider the lasting impact on community or industry by envisioning how your projects can make a positive difference.
- ❖ Infuse purpose and contribution into phases by setting clear intentions for each project's impact.

Seek Support And Accountability

In order to strengthen your commitment to your vision and goals, it is crucial to seek support and accountability from trusted individuals who can play a supportive role in your journey. Sharing your vision and goals with friends, family, or mentors can provide valuable support, encouragement, and guidance as you strive to achieve your long-term aspirations.

Begin by selecting a few individuals whom you trust and respect to share your vision and goals with. These can be close friends, family members, mentors, or even like-minded individuals who share similar aspirations. Openly communicate your dreams and ambitions to them, explaining the importance of their support in your journey.

When sharing your vision and goals, be clear about the level of support you are seeking. Let them know how they can best support you—whether it's through regular check-ins, providing advice and guidance, or simply being a source of motivation and inspiration. Once you clearly articulate the role you envision them playing in your pursuit of long-term success and fulfilment, it will be easier for them to play the roles you require.

When seeking support for your vision and goals, it's important to approach the conversation with authenticity and honesty. Here are some key areas that you should consider genuinely asking for support with:

Share Your Passion And Purpose: Explain why your vision and goals matter to you on a personal level. Help others understand the underlying motivation and significance behind your aspirations.

Be Vulnerable About Your Challenges: Share any fears, doubts, or obstacles you may be facing in pursuing your vision. This vulnerability can create a deeper connection and help others empathize with your journey.

Request Empathy And Understanding: Recognize that not everyone will fully grasp your vision, but ask for their empathy and willingness to listen and support you anyway. Encourage open dialogue and the sharing of diverse perspectives.

Seek Advice And Guidance: Ask for guidance from individuals who have relevant experience or knowledge. Let them know that their insights are valuable to you and that you trust their judgment.

It is important to choose individuals who genuinely believe in you and your potential for growth. Surround yourself with positive influences that uplift and inspire you to keep moving forward, even during challenging times. Seek out mentors or role models who have achieved similar goals or who embody the qualities and values you aspire to cultivate. In the end, your journey is uniquely yours, and the most crucial understanding comes from within but having support along your journey can alleviate pressure when the situation demands.

Engage in regular check-ins with your support network to update them on your progress, challenges, and achievements. These check-ins can be in the form of scheduled meetings, phone calls, or even casual conversations. Use these opportunities to reflect on your journey, seek feedback, and gain insights from their perspectives. Surrounding yourself with individuals who inspire and encourage or communities who share similar goals and aspirations is also essential. Their feedback can provide valuable insights, suggestions, and alternative viewpoints that may enhance your progress and decision-making.

Always remember that seeking support and accountability is not a sign of weakness but rather a demonstration of strength and self-awareness. It takes courage to open up about your dreams and invite others to join you on your journey. Through establishing a support network and embracing accountability, you significantly enhance your ability to stay dedicated, inspired, and resilient as you work towards your long-term vision.

Be sure to express gratitude to those who support you along the way, acknowledging their contributions and celebrating their role in your progress. The journey towards achieving your vision is not a solitary one, and the support and accountability provided by others can be instrumental in your success.

Adapt And Review Regularly

As we navigate the intricate web of experiences, choices, and challenges, it is often in retrospect that we glimpse the hidden threads connecting our journey. In the realm of personal growth and goal attainment, this principle holds particular significance. Our plans, meticulously crafted with vision and purpose, may encounter unforeseen twists and turns along the way. It is during these moments of adaptation and reflection that we come to appreciate the wisdom embedded in hindsight.

Throughout the 15-year plan, periodically reassess your goals to ensure they continue to align with your values and promote personal growth. As you evolve as a person and your circumstances change, it is natural for your goals to evolve as well; you should embrace the opportunity to refine and adjust your goals in response to your personal growth journey. Through regular review and adaptation of our plans, we gain a deeper understanding of our past, embrace the present with heightened clarity, and forge a path towards a future that resonates with our evolving aspirations. The power lies not only in the act of reviewing but also in the ability to glean insights, adjust our course, and grow in wisdom as we embark on the ever-unfolding journey of self-discovery.

Set aside dedicated time at regular intervals to reflect on your progress, reassess your goals, and evaluate their alignment with your aspirations. This review process allows you to gauge whether your goals are still meaningful and relevant to your evolving vision. Consider any changes in your values, interests, or life circumstances that may have occurred since you initially defined your goals.

Be open to new opportunities that may arise or have already revealed themselves along the way. Stay curious and receptive to ideas, experiences, and feedback from others. These new insights may present alternative paths or possibilities that can enhance or reshape your goals. Embrace flexibility and be willing to adjust your plan to accommodate unforeseen circumstances or changing priorities.

When reviewing your goals, ask yourself questions such as:

❖ Have there been any significant changes in my life circumstances or aspirations that require a revision of this goal?
❖ Am I still excited and motivated by this goal, or has it lost its relevance?
❖ Are there new opportunities or experiences that I should consider integrating into my plan?

Based on your reflections and answers to these questions, make intentional adjustments to your goals and action plan. This may involve modifying timelines, refining the scope of certain goals, or even replacing goals that no longer serve your vision. Be mindful of striking a balance between staying committed to your long-term vision and being adaptable to new possibilities.

Remember, adapting and reviewing your plan is not an admission of failure but a demonstration of your willingness to learn and grow. It showcases your commitment to staying aligned with your evolving vision and maximizing your potential for long-term success and fulfilment. By regularly adapting and reviewing your goals, you ensure that your actions remain purposeful, relevant, and in harmony with your aspirations.

Pro Tip: The Priority Pyramid

The Priority Pyramid Framework is a simple and effective method designed to help you prioritize tasks and make decisions with clarity and efficiency. This simplified method, empowers you to make effective decisions, ensuring your day is a balanced blend of productivity and self-care.

How the Priority Pyramid Works:

Divide and Categorize: Begin by dividing your tasks into three distinct categories:

❖ **Base:** These are essential tasks that directly contribute to your primary goals and essential responsibilities.

- ❖ **Middle:** These tasks have a moderate impact and may contribute to your goals indirectly.
- ❖ **Top:** These tasks are optional or have minimal impact on your immediate goals.

Allocate Levels: Assign each task a level based on its priority and importance. The levels correspond to the categories you've defined:

- ❖ **Base (Level 1):** Tasks that align directly with your key goals or responsibilities.
- ❖ **Middle (Level 2):** Tasks that are significant but not as crucial as Level 1 tasks.
- ❖ **Top (Level 3):** Tasks that are less urgent or have lower impact.

Build the Pyramid: Create a visual pyramid on paper or digitally. The pyramid's base represents Level 1 tasks, the middle section represents Level 2 tasks, and the top represents Level 3 tasks.

Prioritize Within Levels: Within each level, arrange tasks based on their urgency. Tasks at the top of each level should be tackled first.

Focus on the Base: Start by addressing tasks in the Base category. These are your top priorities that directly contribute to your goals.

Manage Middle and Top: After completing your Base tasks, move on to the Middle category. Once Middle tasks are addressed, you can choose whether to tackle Top tasks or defer them to a more suitable time.

Benefits of the Priority Pyramid Framework:

- ❖ **Simplicity:** The Pyramid's three-tier structure is easy to understand and apply, making it accessible for anyone.
- ❖ **Quick Decision-Making:** The Pyramid helps you swiftly categorize tasks, allowing you to make decisions efficiently.
- ❖ **Focused Execution:** Concentrating on Base tasks first ensure that your essential goals are being actively pursued.
- ❖ **Reduced Overwhelm:** Breaking tasks into categories and levels reduces the feeling of being overwhelmed by a long list of tasks.

❖ **Flexible Adaptation:** The framework allows you to adapt as priorities change, ensuring your focus remains aligned with your goals.

Example Pyramid:

Base (Level 1):

- ❖ Complete work presentation
- ❖ Review budget proposal
- ❖ Attend important meeting
- ❖ Get 30 New Leads
- ❖ Prepare healthy meals

Middle (Level 2):

- ❖ Research industry trends for project
- ❖ Follow up on pending emails
- ❖ Quick grocery shopping after work

Top (Level 3):

- ❖ Gym session for physical well-being
- ❖ Organize workspace for the next day
- ❖ Read industry news for leisure
- ❖ Engage in a relaxing evening meditation

Using the Priority Pyramid, you'd start by completing the Level 1 tasks first to ensure that your primary goals are met. Then, you can address Level 2 tasks and decide if you have time to tackle any Level 3 tasks.

The Priority Pyramid empowers you to make informed decisions about how to spend your time and energy, ultimately helping you achieve your goals more effectively.

Chapter Summary

In this transformative chapter, we've delved deep into the concept of phases within your 15-year plan, and how they are not just steps but building blocks. By breaking down your aspirations into manageable segments, you're essentially crafting your life's masterpiece, piece by piece. These phases serve as your guiding stars, providing direction, focus, and a sense of purpose.

Seeking accountability within each phase is an essential aspect of this journey. Sharing your vision and goals with trusted individuals, whether they be friends, family, mentors, or like-minded peers, can provide invaluable support, guidance, and motivation. It's a way to anchor your commitment and create a network of encouragement around your aspirations.

To enhance your productivity and maintain a balanced approach to your goals, we introduced the Priority Pyramid framework. This simple yet effective method categorizes tasks into levels of importance and urgency, helping you make efficient decisions about how to allocate your time and energy. Understand that building your future takes time, patience, and dedication. But with each block you place, you're shaping a future that's not only substantial but also aligned with your deepest desires.

Each phase of the action plan presents unique opportunities for skill development, knowledge acquisition, and personal transformation. By allocating time and resources and setting goals within each phase, you continuously build the foundation needed to reach your long-term goals. Viewing your journey as a series of interconnected phases allows you to incorporate valuable insights and course corrections from one stage into the next.

By breaking down your bigger picture into smaller steps, you learn how to effectively execute your complete vision. This approach provides day-by-day, week-by-week, and month-by-month action plans, ensuring continuous progress.

Ultimately, your 15-year plan is more than just a document or ideas on paper; it's your legacy in the making. It's a living testament to your ambition, resilience, and determination. As you progress through each phase, you're not just inching closer to your dreams; you're actively living them. And it's through this journey, this meticulous stacking of building blocks, that you will discover not only the depth of your potential but the extraordinary heights to which you can ascend. So, embrace each phase, not as a mere step but as a vital component of your life's architectural design.

A New Phase

Congratulations! You have reached the end of the planning phase, where you have returned to ground zero, gained clarity on your vision, set meaningful goals, and outlined a strategic roadmap for the next 15 years. You now stand at the threshold of an exciting new chapter - the action phase, where you will bring your plans to life and build the future you envision.

Just as a foundation is essential for a sturdy structure, the planning phase has provided you with a solid groundwork. You have taken the time to reflect on who you are, where you want to go, and what steps are required to get there. This valuable self-discovery process has equipped you with the knowledge, insights, and motivation needed to embark on the journey of building your dreams.

From Vision to Reality

Now, it's time to transition from motion to action. The plans you have carefully crafted are meant to be realized, and the steps you have outlined are waiting to be taken. It's important to remember that progress is not achieved by simply thinking or talking about your goals; it comes from rolling up your sleeves and doing the real work. As you embark on this action phase, keep in mind that building your dreams requires dedication, perseverance, and a willingness to embrace both successes and setbacks.

In the upcoming chapters, we will dive into the practical steps and skills required to turn your plans into tangible results. You will learn how to mould public perception to your goals, create financial discipline and build a mindset with resilience at its core. Stay focused on your goals, maintain a growth mindset, and be open to learning from every experience, remembering that building your future is not a linear journey; it's a continuous process of learning, evolving, and refining your approach.

Now is the time to take the leap, to step into action, and to build the future you have envisioned. Your plans are no longer just ideas on paper; they are seeds waiting to be planted and nurtured. Embrace the excitement and challenges that lie ahead, and trust in your abilities to create the life you desire.

As we conclude this phase, remember that your journey is **_unique and personal._** Stay true to your values, remain committed to your vision, and let your actions speak louder than words. With every step you take, you are not only building a brighter future for yourself but also inspiring others to pursue their own dreams.

You're now at a pivotal point in 'The 15 Year Plan', transitioning from meticulous planning to dynamic action. To support you in this exciting phase of turning your vision into reality, we encourage you to utilize our free online resources.

These additional tools are tailored to help you apply the concepts you've learned and navigate the upcoming challenges effectively. They offer practical advice, tips, and strategies that align with the action steps you're about to undertake. Remember, the journey from planning to action is enriched with continuous learning and adaptation. These resources are here to guide you every step of the way as you build and shape the future you envision.

PART 2:
FROM VISION
TO REALITY

CHAPTER 4:
FINANCIAL HEALTH

Financial Health

Financial health is not just about money; it's about gaining wisdom to make the resources you have work for you. Just as your physical, spiritual and mental wellbeing needs care, your finances, the very tool that powers your ambitions, requires a dedication to maintain a healthy and sustainable state.

First, you need a strong foundation I.e, financial literacy. It's about understanding your money: how to save, invest, and grow it. Financial Literacy is the cornerstone of a successful financial framework and serves as the bedrock for making informed and strategic financial decisions. Think of financial literacy as your toolkit. Just as a carpenter needs to know when to use a hammer or a wrench, understanding the basics of money helps you make smart decisions. Whether you're figuring out how to handle an unexpected bill or deciding where to invest, this knowledge is key.

Financial health involves a commitment to continuously learn and understanding the principles of personal finance, investing, and wealth-building strategies. Investing in your financial education equips you with the knowledge and skills necessary to optimize your cash flow, secure your financial future, and achieve your long-term financial goals. Investing in your financial education is like having a map for a busy high street. There are countless stores, each offering something different. If you don't know what you're looking for, you might feel overwhelmed. But, if you've taken some time to learn and understand your needs, you can navigate it confidently. You'll know which "stores" (or investment opportunities) to visit and which to avoid. You'll recognize when something is a real deal or just too risky for you.

Financial literacy empowers you to make informed decisions that align with your unique financial goals and risk tolerance. It allows you to assess different investment opportunities, evaluate their potential risks and rewards, and select strategies that align with your long-term objectives. Armed with financial knowledge, you can avoid common pitfalls, identify opportunities for growth, and develop a prudent approach to managing or creating cash flow.

As your circumstances evolve, your financial goals may shift, requiring you to adapt your strategies accordingly. Staying up to date with the latest trends, regulations, and best practices ensures that your financial framework remains relevant and effective throughout the 15-year plan. Be informed and you can proactively adjust your financial plan to accommodate changing priorities.

The Distinction Between Salary, Revenue, And Income

It is imperative to grasp the nuanced differences between salary, revenue, and income. These terms, often used interchangeably, hold distinct meanings that significantly impact one's financial well-being and fiscal planning. When looking deeper into their definitions and implications, individuals gain a comprehensive understanding of their financial health and develop effective strategies to achieve financial goals.

First and foremost, let's clarify the concept of salary. Salary is the fixed compensation an individual receives from their employer for services rendered. It is typically stated as an annual amount, divided into regular pay periods, such as monthly or biweekly. This fixed income provides financial stability and serves as a foundation for managing day-to-day expenses. However, it is essential to recognize that a salary is not synonymous with income in its entirety.

Revenue, on the other hand, encompasses the total inflow of funds from all sources, including but not limited to a salary. It comprises various streams of income, such as earnings from self-employment, freelance work, investments, rental properties, or any other sources of financial gains. Revenue constitutes the gross earnings before any deductions or expenses are accounted for, reflecting the overall financial inflow.

To attain a comprehensive understanding of one's financial standing, the critical factor to consider is the derivation of net income. Net income represents the amount remaining after subtracting all expenses from the total revenue. Expenses encompass a wide range of financial obligations, from the mundane costs of daily living, such as rent or mortgage payments, utility bills, groceries, transportation, and insurance, to more substantial financial commitments, such as loan payments or credit card bills.

It is essential to differentiate between discretionary and non-discretionary expenses. Non-discretionary expenses are essential for sustaining one's basic needs and lifestyle, while discretionary expenses are those that can be adjusted or eliminated, such as entertainment or leisure activities. Managing expenses wisely can significantly impact an individual's net income, determining how much can be saved, invested, or utilized for financial goals and aspirations.

Understanding the interplay between salary, revenue, expenses, and net income enables you to make informed financial decisions. Merely focusing on salary alone may lead to financial myopia, overlooking potential sources of revenue or neglecting to consider various expenses that can impact the bottom line.

Action Plan For Financial Prudence

Arming yourself with an action plan is more than just following a series of steps. It is your partner in aligning your financial resources with your life's objectives and ensuring the security of your financial future. At its core, it underscores the pivotal role of regular evaluation and adaptation to seamlessly accommodate life's inevitable changes.

Step 1: Assess Your Current Financial Situation

- ❖ Gather all financial documents, including bank statements, pay stubs, investment statements, and bills.
- ❖ Calculate your total monthly income from all sources, including salaries, bonuses, investments, rental income, and any other revenue streams.
- ❖ List all your fixed expenses, such as rent/mortgage, utilities, insurance premiums, and loan payments.
- ❖ Identify variable expenses, such as groceries, dining out, entertainment, and discretionary spending.

Step 2: Define Your Financial Goals

- ❖ Refer to your goals and vision you set out earlier, this will give you a strong indicator as to what direction you need to be building your finances toward
- ❖ Prioritize your goals based on their importance and timeline.

Step 3: Create A Comprehensive Budget

- ❖ Utilize budgeting tools or apps to organize your income and expenses effectively.
- ❖ Allocate funds for each category, ensuring you include savings and investments as part of your budget.
- ❖ Consider creating separate budget categories for different financial goals.

Step 4: Monitor And Track Expenses

- ❖ Set a regular schedule for reviewing and updating your budget, such as weekly or monthly.
- ❖ Keep track of all your expenses diligently, including small purchases, by using expense tracking apps or software.
- ❖ Categorize your expenses accurately to identify areas for potential cost-cutting.

Step 5: Optimize Your Cash Flow

- ❖ Analyse your budget to identify areas where you can reduce expenses without compromising your priorities.
- ❖ Consider negotiating bills, seeking cost-effective alternatives, or cutting down on discretionary spending.
- ❖ Redirect the saved funds towards your financial goals, such as debt repayment or investments.

Step 6: Cultivate Financial Discipline

- ❖ Commit to following your budget and staying accountable to your financial goals.

- ❖ Avoid impulsive spending by taking time to evaluate purchases and align them with your priorities.
- ❖ Review your progress regularly and celebrate milestones achieved on your financial journey.

Step 7: Evaluate Investment Opportunities

- ❖ Educate yourself about various investment options, such as stocks, bonds, real estate, and retirement accounts.
- ❖ Consult with a financial advisor to assess the suitability of investments based on your risk tolerance and financial goals.
- ❖ Make informed decisions about where to allocate your savings for optimal returns.

Step 8: Reassess And Adjust

- ❖ Life circumstances change, and your financial goals may evolve over time. Regularly reassess your budget and financial plan to accommodate any changes.
- ❖ Be flexible and adjust your budget as needed while staying committed to your long-term aspirations.

There is no point in planning and then not following through. Diligently follow your action plan for budgeting and expense management, to gain control over your financial resources, optimize your cash flow, and work towards achieving your long-term financial goals. Remember that financial prudence is an ongoing process, and each step taken today contributes to a prosperous and fulfilling 15-year journey of financial success and personal growth.

Emergency Funds

Having an emergency fund and contingency planning are crucial for financial stability. An emergency fund should cover six to twelve months of living expenses, acting as a safety net during unforeseen situations like job loss or medical emergencies. It provides peace of mind and prevents falling into debt. Contingency planning goes beyond this fund, identifying risks and finding strategies to mitigate them. Insurance policies and diversification help manage uncertainties. For individuals and businesses, preparation through these measures safeguards financial well-being and allows confident pursuit of long-term goals. With resilience and determination, you can navigate life's uncertainties and maintain control over your financial future.

Simple Equation to Start Saving:

- ❖ **Calculate Monthly Living Expenses**: Add up all your essential monthly expenses, including rent/mortgage, utilities, food, transportation, and insurance.
- ❖ **Set Your Target**: Multiply your monthly expenses by the number of months you want to cover (6-12 months). This is your emergency fund goal. *(Emergency Fund Target = Monthly Living Expenses X Number of months)*
- ❖ **Start Saving**: Begin by setting aside a manageable portion of your income each month towards this fund. Even small contributions can add up over time.

Debt Management

The consequences of poor debt management can be daunting, from compounding interest that threatens your financial stability to the burden of overwhelming debt that stifles your aspirations. However, when approached wisely, debt management becomes a powerful tool, enabling you to reclaim control over your finances and chart a course towards lasting financial freedom.

Once you've identified your debts, it's crucial to prioritize repayment. High-interest debts, such as credit card balances, typically impose significant financial strain due to their compounding interest rates. As such, directing extra payments towards high-interest debts is a prudent strategy to minimize interest costs and expedite debt repayment.

Consistency is key in debt management. Establishing a disciplined approach to making regular payments ensures that debts are steadily reduced over time. Creating a budget that allocates a portion of your income towards debt repayment can be instrumental in maintaining a consistent and structured approach.

Debt optimization is another aspect to consider in the debt management process. This involves exploring opportunities to reduce interest costs and improve debt terms. For instance, you may consider consolidating your high-interest credit card debts into a single loan with a lower interest rate. Refinancing existing loans at more favourable terms can also lead to significant interest savings.

You can also leverage balance transfer options with promotional zero or low-interest rates to temporarily consolidate your credit card debts and reduce interest costs during the promotional period. However, it is essential to be cautious with balance transfers and carefully read the terms and conditions to avoid hidden fees or interest spikes after the promotional period ends.

As you progress through your plan, debt management becomes instrumental in improving your financial well-being and unlocking opportunities for asset accumulation and wealth-building. Reducing your debt burden frees up financial resources, allowing you to redirect funds towards investments, savings, and other ventures that contribute to long-term financial success.

By strategically managing and prioritizing debt repayment, you can alleviate financial stress, minimize interest costs, and work towards achieving a debt-free future. Furthermore, exploring opportunities for debt optimization allows you to leverage more favourable terms, reducing interest expenses and freeing up resources for asset accumulation and wealth-building endeavours. Embracing a disciplined approach to debt management empowers you to take control of your financial destiny and maximize your potential for financial prosperity over the next 15 years and beyond.

Diversifying Income

Exploring various avenues to generate income, can create a robust and resilient cash flow that not only sustains your lifestyle but also fosters wealth creation and financial freedom.

The first step in diversifying income streams is to recognize the limitations of relying solely on a primary job or business for income. While steady employment or successful entrepreneurship provides a stable foundation, it also carries inherent risks, such as job instability or business fluctuations. Diversifying your income streams, can hedge against these risks and insulate yourself from unexpected financial challenges.

Side hustles and freelancing are excellent ways to supplement your primary income and explore alternative revenue sources. You can leverage your skills, talents, or hobbies to offer services or products on a part-time basis, generating additional income. Whether it's freelance writing, graphic design, photography, or consulting, side hustles enable you to monetize your passions and expand your earning potential.

Passive income sources are another key aspect of income diversification. Passive income refers to money earned with minimal active effort, often generated from investments or ventures that require little day-to-day involvement. Investments in stocks, bonds, mutual funds, or real estate can yield dividends, interest, or rental income, providing a steady stream of passive revenue.

Rental properties, in particular, are a popular option for generating passive income. Owning real estate and renting it out to tenants can create a reliable and recurring income stream. However, it is essential to conduct thorough research and due diligence before investing in real estate to ensure that the properties align with your financial goals and risk tolerance.

You can also explore other sources of passive income, such as royalties from creative works like books, music, or digital products. Licensing intellectual property can provide ongoing income, especially in the digital age, where content can be easily distributed and monetized.

Additional income streams provide extra capital that can be directed towards savings, investments, and debt reduction. As multiple income sources grow and compound over time, the potential for accelerated wealth creation becomes evident.

It is essential to approach income diversification with a prudent and well-considered strategy. Rather than pursuing every available opportunity, focus on income streams that align with your skills, interests, and long-term financial goals. Striking a balance between active and passive income sources is also crucial, as active income provides immediate cash flow while passive income offers long-term financial benefits.

Income diversification not only provides additional financial security but also accelerates wealth-building and unlocks the potential for lasting prosperity over the next 15 years and beyond. Embracing diverse income streams empowers you to seize opportunities, weather financial challenges, and embark on a journey towards financial freedom and fulfilment.

Tax Planning

Taking a proactive approach to tax planning, you can maximize tax benefits, minimize liabilities, and retain more of your hard-earned income for savings, investments, and wealth-building endeavours.

The initial step in tax planning is to gain a comprehensive understanding of the tax laws and regulations relevant to your financial situation. Tax laws can differ based on various factors, such as income level, marital status, and revenue sources. Seeking guidance from tax professionals, like certified public accountants (CPAs) or tax advisors, can provide valuable insights into the nuances of tax planning and ensure compliance with all applicable tax laws.

An essential objective of tax planning is to leverage tax-efficient investment vehicles. Certain accounts, such as Individual Savings Accounts (ISAs) or retirement accounts, offer tax advantages that can effectively reduce your tax liabilities. Contributing to these accounts allows you to benefit from tax-free growth or deferred taxation, depending on the account type.

Tax planning involves strategically maximizing deductions and credits to lower taxable income. Deductions for charitable contributions, mortgage interest, and education expenses can all contribute to reducing your overall taxable income, resulting in a diminished tax liability. Likewise, tax credits provide a direct reduction in the tax owed, offering significant savings on tax payments.

Staying informed about changes in tax laws is crucial, and tax professionals are adept at identifying new opportunities for tax optimization. Engaging with tax experts ensures that you remain up to date with the latest tax strategies and can capitalize on any new tax incentives or provisions.

Structuring income and expenses strategically is another aspect of tax optimization. Timing certain income to a later year or accelerating deductible expenses can help optimize your tax liability in any given tax year. Careful consideration of the timing of capital gains and losses on investments can also impact tax planning.

Compliance with tax laws is essential while seeking to maximize tax benefits. Accountants and tax professionals can guide you through the complexities of tax compliance and identify areas where tax savings can be maximized within legal boundaries.

Optimizing tax planning can significantly impact your overall financial standing. Reduced tax liabilities translate to more funds available for savings and investments, accelerating your wealth-building efforts over time.

By utilizing tax-efficient investment options, maximizing deductions and credits, and seeking guidance from tax professionals, you can optimize your tax planning and create a solid foundation for wealth-building and financial success over the next 15 years and beyond.

Retirement Planning

With each stride through the various chapters of life, the significance of a well-constructed retirement plan becomes increasingly evident. As we navigate the intricate landscape of long-term financial planning, retirement and securing our financial well-being for the years beyond our 15-year journey stand as a pivotal cornerstone of one's financial health.

As you progress through different stages of life, having a well-thought-out retirement plan becomes essential. Contributing to retirement accounts or Individual Retirement Accounts (IRAs) allows you to take advantage of tax advantages and accumulate funds for your retirement years. Allocating a portion of your income towards retirement savings is a prudent step to ensure financial stability in your later years.

Consulting with financial advisors and retirement specialists can be beneficial in crafting a comprehensive retirement and long-term plan. These professionals can help you assess your financial situation, determine your retirement needs, and develop strategies to achieve your long-term goals. They can also assist you in identifying suitable investment opportunities and guide you through any necessary adjustments to your plan as circumstances change.

When considering retirement planning, it is essential to define specific retirement goals. Determine the age at which you plan to retire and the lifestyle you wish to maintain during retirement. Having clear and realistic retirement goals will enable you to calculate the required amount of savings and tailor your contributions accordingly.

Retirement and long-term planning require consistent review and adjustment as your life evolves. As you progress through different life stages, your financial goals and circumstances may change, necessitating modifications to your plan. Regularly reassessing your retirement and long-term goals with the help of financial experts can help you stay on track and ensure that your financial plan aligns with your evolving needs and aspirations.

Embracing retirement and long-term planning as essential elements of your financial journey empowers you to build a solid foundation for financial security and success well beyond the next 15 years. Taking proactive steps now will empower you to enjoy a comfortable retirement and leave a lasting legacy for generations to come.

Legacy Planning

Legacy planning and wealth transfer strategies are equally significant components of long-term planning. Legacy planning involves creating a plan for the transfer of your assets and wealth to your beneficiaries or chosen charitable causes after your passing. Being thoughtful with your legacy planning, means you ensure your hard-earned assets are distributed according to your wishes, minimizing potential conflicts, and preserving family harmony.

Various estate planning tools, such as wills, trusts, and power of attorney documents, are essential for executing effective legacy planning. Working with legal professionals who specialize in estate planning can help ensure that your estate is managed efficiently, and your beneficiaries receive their inheritances with minimum tax implications and legal complications.

Considering wealth transfer strategies ensures that the next generation can benefit from the assets you have accumulated over time. This may involve initiating gifting strategies during your lifetime or utilizing trusts to protect and distribute assets to future generations. The goal is to create a smooth and tax-efficient transfer of wealth, allowing your loved ones to benefit from your hard work and financial success.

A crucial aspect of long-term financial planning is regularly reassessing and adjusting your strategies. Life circumstances, financial goals, and market conditions can change over time, necessitating adjustments to your financial plans. Review regularly and update your financial strategies, to ensure that your long-term planning remains relevant and effective.

It is essential to recognize that cash, while providing temporary security, does not possess the ability to generate lasting wealth. The true power lies in acquiring and growing assets that have the potential to appreciate over time. Equity, whether in real estate, stocks, businesses, or other investments, holds the key to significant returns, building your net worth, and securing your financial future. By shifting your focus towards acquiring assets, you transform from being solely a consumer of goods and services to becoming an investor in your own success.

To realize the full potential of equity and wealth-building, investment stands as the cornerstone of the journey. Rather than letting your hard-earned money sit idle in a savings account, putting it to work through strategic investments can lead to exponential growth. Diversifying your investment portfolio is key to mitigating risk and capitalizing on diverse opportunities. Stocks, bonds, real estate, and other ventures each offer unique advantages and risk profiles.

Building substantial wealth through equity and investment requires patience and a long-term vision. Compounding, the snowball effect of reinvesting earnings, accelerates over time. As your assets grow, they generate even more returns, leading to a self-sustaining cycle of wealth creation. This compounding phenomenon is most powerful when given the luxury of time. Remaining committed to your investment strategies and staying the course, allows you to truly harness the full potential of long-term compounding and experience substantial growth.

As your journey towards wealth and prosperity unfolds, consider the impact you wish to leave on the world. Giving back through philanthropy can be an immensely fulfilling aspect of your financial journey. Whether supporting charitable causes, community initiatives, or projects aligned with your values, giving back allows you to leave a positive legacy and make a meaningful difference in the lives of others.

Equity, investments, and lifelong learning together form the foundation for your path to lasting wealth and a purposeful life. Through shifting your focus from cash to acquiring and growing assets, you unlock the potential for significant returns and financial security. Adopt a spirit of entrepreneurship regardless of your chosen career path, to create your route to success, and approach your financial journey with patience, long-term vision, and adaptability. Embracing these principles empowers you to embark on a fulfilling 15-year journey towards lasting wealth and a life of purpose and abundance.

Chapter Summary

As we wrap up this chapter, we're concluding our deep dive into financial well-being—a task that lays the foundation for a future filled with prosperity. Our exploration began by recognizing the vital role of financial literacy—a set of tools essential for making sound money decisions. Think of it as a baseline for understanding your finances, enabling us to navigate unexpected expenses and make informed investment choices.

We delved into the significance of distinguishing between salary, revenue, and income, understanding that a comprehensive financial picture encompasses all revenue streams. The management of both essential and discretionary expenses shapes our net income, guiding us toward potential savings and investment avenues. Our pragmatic approach to financial prudence provided us with actionable steps: evaluating our financial situation, defining clear goals, creating workable budgets, diligently tracking expenses, optimizing cash flow, and making well-informed investment decisions.

The spotlight then shifted to debt management—an area that guides us to prioritize paying off high-interest debts while optimizing the management of debt in general. This strategy releases funds that can be channelled into investments, propelling us toward a path of financial liberation. Furthermore, we explored diversifying our income sources, from side hustles and freelancing to passive income generated through investments. This diversification not only strengthens our financial foundation but also accelerates the process of wealth creation. In parallel, we grasped the importance of effective tax planning, maximizing benefits while minimizing financial liabilities by strategically leveraging investments and deductions.

As we moved forward, we understood that retirement planning acts as a bridge to a secure and comfortable future. Contributing to retirement accounts and seeking expert advice ensures a cushion of financial stability as we journey through life. Legacy planning came into play, allowing us to protect our assets and wealth, leaving a meaningful legacy for the generations to come. Equity and investments emerged as our tools for wealth building, with diverse portfolios that drive financial growth through compounding effects.

In essence, this chapter underscores the transformative power of knowledge and strategic action. Weaving these principles into our financial journey, we pave the way for growth, security, and a future imbued with meaningful abundance. Reflect on the information, adapt them to your life's twists and turns, and let them guide you towards a future brimming with financial success and the fulfilment of your dreams.

CHAPTER 5: DEVELOPING YOUR PERSONAL BRAND IDENTITY

Developing Your Personal Brand

In the 15-Year Success Plan, the next step is to develop your personal brand, which is how you are perceived by others in both personal and professional settings. A strong personal brand requires authenticity, consistency, and clarity. Being authentic means staying true to yourself, being honest, and presenting yourself transparently. Consistency means presenting a consistent image and message across all platforms and interactions. Clarity means being clear about your values, what you stand for, and what you have to offer.

To create a strong personal brand, you need to first identify how you want to be perceived by others. This involves building upon your core values, beliefs, and unique strengths. You can ask yourself questions such as:

- ❖ **What do I stand for?**
- ❖ **What are my unique qualities?**
- ❖ **What are my strengths and skills?**
- ❖ **What do I want to define my legacy?**

The majority of your answers will be gleaned from the personal audit in the first step of the 15-year plan. Once you have identified these key elements, you can use them to develop a consistent personal brand that is reflected in your social media presence, networking activities, and professional interactions. Your personal brand should reflect your values, beliefs, unique strengths, skills, and experiences. It is a crucial aspect of your success as it can help you attract the right opportunities and people into your life.

Establish A Consistent Visual Style: Determine a consistent visual style that aligns with your personality and resonates with your target audience. Consider aspects such as colour palette, typography, graphic elements, and overall aesthetics. This consistent visual style should be reflected across all your online platforms, including your website, social media profiles, and promotional materials.

Quality Imagery: Invest in high-quality images that showcase your personality, expertise, and unique qualities. These images should be used consistently across your personal branding materials, allowing people to easily recognize you and connect with your brand. With advancements in modern technology, we can create a lot of imagery from the phones in our pockets.

Visual Branding Assets: Create a set of visual branding assets, such as a logo, iconography, and brand patterns, which reflect your personal brand and can be used consistently across all your digital and printed materials. These assets should be designed to enhance recognition and reinforce your brand's identity.

Curate Social Media Profiles: Optimize your social media profiles by aligning them with your visual identity. Use professional profile pictures, consistent cover photos, and visually appealing graphics that represent your brand. This visual consistency across platforms helps build a strong personal brand image.

Showcase Your Expertise: Highlight your best work or projects through a portfolio, social media sharing, case studies, or artistic creations. Demonstrate your capabilities and style to potential clients, customers, or collaborators.

Provide Informative Content: Offer detailed information about your services, products, rates, or availability. This builds trust, credibility, and enables informed decision-making. Explain your expertise, process, or creative approach to give others a clear understanding of what you bring to the table.

Showcase Your Personal Style: Your personal style should align with your brand identity and target audience. Pay attention to how you present yourself through your clothing, accessories, and overall appearance. Ensure that your style reflects the image you want to portray to your audience.

Engage Authentically: Be genuine and authentic in your interactions with your audience. Engage with them through visual content, such as photos, videos, and live streams, which showcases your personality and expertise. Encourage conversation and respond to comments or messages in a timely and authentic manner.

Foster A Sense Of Community: Encourage your audience to feel like they are part of your brand by creating a sense of community. This can be achieved through merchandise, fan events, social media engagement, and other methods that bring your audience closer to your brand. Building a loyal community fosters a sense of belonging and loyalty among your fans and followers.

Embrace Collaboration: Look for opportunities to collaborate with other professionals who share your vision and can help expand your brand. This could include joint projects, co-branding, or sharing resources and ideas. Collaboration opens up new possibilities and exposes your brand to new audiences. Attend industry events, conferences, or networking opportunities to connect with like-minded professionals and potential collaborators. Collaborations can help expand your personal brand's reach and introduce you to new audiences.

Maintain Consistency: Ensure that your branding, messaging, and visual identity are consistent across all of your online platforms. This establishes a strong personal brand and makes it easier for potential clients, customers, or collaborators to recognize and remember you.

Iterate and Innovate: Constantly seek fresh ideas and creative avenues, whether through experimenting with new formats, exploring uncharted markets, or daringly expanding your brand's thematic scope. Such continuous innovation ensures relevance and captivates your audience. Simultaneously, invest in your personal and professional growth to enhance your skills and knowledge. This not only positions you as an authority in your field but also fuels the evolution and resilience of your brand. Remember, in the ever-changing landscape of branding, a commitment to iteration and innovation is key to maintaining vibrancy and engagement.

Pro Tip: Public Perception And Reputation

The importance of managing one's public perception within an industry cannot be overstated. How others perceive you within your professional sphere directly impacts your reputation, credibility, and relationships with peers and colleagues. Building a positive industry reputation and earning the respect of others are crucial elements in achieving long-term success in your career.

While it is true that your skills and expertise are essential, how you are perceived by others can significantly influence opportunities, collaborations, and advancement in your field. Managing your public perception allows you to shape your professional identity, establish a strong personal brand, and position yourself as a valuable and respected authority within your industry.

Your Industry Identifier: Identify the core principles, and professional attributes that define who you are within your industry. Understand the qualities that set you apart and contribute to your unique professional identity. This will shape the way others perceive you and form the basis of your industry reputation.

Establish A Professional Online Presence: Though you may not aim for a public personal brand, having a professional online presence is essential for industry recognition. Create a LinkedIn profile and ensure it showcases your experience, achievements, and expertise. Keep your online presence updated and engage in relevant industry discussions and forums. This way, you can establish credibility and be seen as a knowledgeable professional within your field.

Build Relationships And Network: Cultivate meaningful connections within your industry by attending workshops, seminars, and industry events. Engage in conversations, participate in panels or conferences, and seek opportunities to collaborate with others. Building strong relationships with industry peers not only enhances your professional network but also contributes to your industry reputation.

Be Visible And Active: Even if you prefer to maintain a low public profile, being active and visible within your industry is important. Share your insights, thoughts, and expertise through industry publications, forums, or professional groups. This can be done by writing articles, contributing to industry blogs, or speaking at industry-related events. By sharing valuable knowledge and insights, you can enhance your reputation as a respected professional.

Seek Industry Recognition: While you may not actively pursue public personal branding, receiving recognition within your industry can positively impact how others perceive you. Utilize awards, nominations, or accolades that acknowledge your contributions and expertise. This recognition enhances your credibility and reinforces your standing within the industry.

Foster A Reputation For Excellence: Maintain a consistent focus on delivering high-quality work and displaying professionalism in all your endeavours. Consistently meeting and exceeding industry standards will earn you a reputation for excellence. This reputation will be noticed and respected by others in your industry, enhancing your professional standing and perception.

Demonstrate Continuous Improvement: Invest in your professional growth and stay updated with industry trends, advancements, and best practices. Showcase your commitment to continuous learning and professional development. Demonstrating a thirst for knowledge and sharing what you learn, positions you as a valuable asset within your industry.

Seek Mentors And Guidance: Identify experienced professionals within your industry who can serve as mentors or guides. Their guidance can help you navigate challenges, offer valuable insights, and provide opportunities for growth. Building relationships with industry veterans demonstrates your commitment to personal and professional development, further enhancing your reputation within the industry.

Maintain Professionalism and Integrity: Above all, uphold professionalism and integrity in all your interactions and endeavours. Demonstrating ethical conduct and a strong moral compass earns the respect and trust of others within your industry. Consistently acting with integrity enhances your reputation and solidifies the positive perception others have of you.

While maintaining a public personal brand may not be your goal, the perception of others within your industry is still essential and something you want to be in control of.

Imposter Syndrome

We find ourselves in an era where the relentless stream of information provides us with a front-row seat to witness the culmination of everyone's achievements. The constant visibility of others' accomplishments can evoke a range of emotions within us - inspiration, envy, motivation, or self-doubt. In this age of hyper-connectivity, it is not uncommon for individuals to grapple with a phenomenon known as Imposter Syndrome.

Imposter Syndrome is a deeply ingrained sense of self-doubt and fear of being exposed as a fraud, despite one's accomplishments and capabilities. Those affected by this internal struggle often attribute their success to luck or external factors, downplaying their own skills and hard work. They constantly compare themselves to others, particularly those they see on social media, fuelling their feelings of inadequacy and self-doubt.

It can affect anyone, regardless of their background, accomplishments, or expertise. High-achieving professionals, creative artists, and even those in leadership positions often wrestle with feelings of inadequacy and self-doubt. It stems from the fear of being perceived as incompetent or unworthy, despite evidence to the contrary.

Overcoming Imposter Syndrome

The first step towards overcoming Imposter Syndrome is recognizing its presence in your life. Acknowledge that these feelings of self-doubt and fear are not uncommon and that they do not accurately reflect your true abilities. Understand that many accomplished individuals have experienced similar doubts, which reinforces the fact that Imposter Syndrome is not an accurate reflection of your worth.

Once you've acknowledged Imposter Syndrome, challenge the negative self-talk that perpetuates it. Replace self-defeating thoughts with empowering and realistic affirmations. Remind yourself of your past achievements, the skills you possess, and the hard work you have put into honing your expertise. Celebrate your successes and recognize that they are a testament to your capabilities, not mere coincidences. Reflecting on your answers, to limiting beliefs within the Personal Audit, may just have revealed the exact parts of your life triggering the feeling of being an imposter.

To tackle Imposter Syndrome, step outside your own perspective and seek insight from trusted friends, mentors, or colleagues. Discussing your self-doubt with them can provide a much-needed objective view, highlighting your strengths and achievements. This supportive network can effectively counter the negative self-talk, offering a realistic and positive reflection of your abilities.

Recognize that no one knows everything, and it's natural to have areas where you can improve. Instead of viewing mistakes or challenges as confirmation of your perceived incompetence, see them as opportunities for growth and development. Adopt a growth mindset that embraces challenges as steppingstones to mastery.

It's important to remember that Imposter Syndrome is not a measure of your worth or competence. Instead of striving for perfection, focus on progress and embracing your authentic self. Embrace vulnerability and recognize that it takes courage to be genuine and open about your fears and insecurities.

Lastly, be kind to yourself. Treat yourself with the same compassion and understanding you would extend to a friend facing similar doubts. Understand that experiencing self-doubt does not diminish your worth or negate your achievements. Embrace self-care practices that nourish your mind, body, and spirit, allowing you to build resilience and maintain a positive mindset.

Overcoming Imposter Syndrome is a journey that requires self-reflection, self-compassion, and a commitment to personal growth. By recognizing and challenging the negative thoughts and beliefs that fuel this phenomenon, you can break free from the grip of self-doubt and embrace your true worth. Remember, you are deserving of success and capable of achieving great things.

Pro Tip: Brand Voice

A brand voice is not just a tone or a personality. It's the voice that speaks for you, the embodiment of your business's values and identity. It's how your audience / network perceive you and how you connect with them on an emotional level. It's the bedrock of your brand / reputation, and it's essential for building trust and loyalty.

Here are some key steps to help you develop a strong brand voice for your business:

Know Your Audience: The first step in developing a strong brand voice is to understand your audience. Who are you speaking to? What do your customers care about? What tone and language do they respond to? Conduct market research and gather insights to help you answer these questions.

Define Your Brand Personality: Once you understand your audience, define your brand personality. What are the core values and characteristics that define your brand? Are you playful and light-hearted or serious and authoritative? Use this information to shape your brand voice.

Establish Brand Guidelines: Create brand guidelines that outline the specific tone, language, and style that you will use in your communications. This will help ensure consistency across all touchpoints and make it easier for your team to create content that aligns with your brand voice.

Use Visual Elements To Reinforce Your Brand Voice: Visual elements, such as colour palette and typography, can also help reinforce your brand voice. Choose visual elements that align with your brand personality and use them consistently across all marketing materials.

Test And Refine: Improve your brand voice over time with various iterations. Monitor how your audience responds to your communications and adjust your tone and messaging accordingly. A strong brand voice is one that evolves with your business and audiences find engaging.

A strong brand voice creates a consistent and recognizable identity that sets you apart from your competitors. It helps you establish authority and credibility in your industry and makes it easier for customers to remember and recommend you. But most importantly, a brand voice is a reflection of who you are as a business. It's a way to showcase your values and personality and to connect with your customers on a deeper level.

A brand voice is more than just words and language. It's a reflection of your brand's identity, values, and personality. It's essential for building trust and loyalty, establishing authority and credibility, and creating a lasting impression on your audience. A strong brand voice is a key ingredient to a successful business, and it's worth investing time and effort to develop it.

In our quest for success within the 15-year plan, a strong brand voice becomes an indispensable asset. It serves as a beacon that guides us, differentiates us, and propels us forward. By investing time and effort into its development, we elevate our brand's presence, leaving an indelible mark on our audience and setting the stage for our triumphant journey towards our long-term goals.

Pro Tip: Shop Window

As someone with a personal brand, whether you're a CEO, artist, or freelancer, it is essential to understand and apply the concept of the "shop window" in your online presence, including social media and website. The shop window is an analogy for the way businesses present themselves to potential customers, much like a physical store displays its merchandise in a way that attracts the attention of passers-by. In the context of personal branding, your online presence is your shop window. It is often the first point of contact between you and potential clients, customers, or collaborators, and it is your opportunity to make a strong first impression. It is therefore vital to present yourself in a way that is professional, engaging, and informative.

There are four key benefits to understanding and applying the shop window concept for your personal brand:

Attracting Opportunities: Your online presence serves as your shop window, attracting potential clients, customers, investors, or collaborators to your services or projects. Presenting yourself professionally and showcase your skills, experience, or artistic portfolio, can draw in opportunities that may not have found you otherwise.

Establishing Credibility: A well-designed and informative online presence can help establish your credibility. This is particularly important for those who want to build trust and a positive reputation in their respective fields. Sharing your expertise, builds on your previous accomplishments and past successes, creating credibility and gaining the trust of potential partners or clients.

Demonstrating Expertise: Your online presence can be used to showcase your expertise in your field. This can include sharing examples of your work, projects, or initiatives, creating insightful content such as blog posts or videos related to your industry or artistic practice, or providing testimonials from satisfied clients, customers, or collaborators. Demonstrating your expertise helps position you as a go-to authority in your area of specialization.

Building A Strong Personal Brand: Your online presence plays a crucial role in building a personal brand. This involves creating a consistent visual identity across all of your online platforms, developing a unique voice and tone for your content, and expressing your values, mission, or artistic style. A strong personal brand helps you differentiate yourself and leaves a lasting impression on your audience.

By presenting yourself professionally, showcasing your skills, and engaging with your audience, you can create a compelling online presence that attracts opportunities, establishes credibility, and distinguishes you in your field.

Chapter Summary

In this chapter, we delved into the critical topic of personal brand development and its significance within the context of your plan. We explored essential aspects such as brand image, authenticity, and the impact of our public perception on our long-term vision and goals.

We recognized the importance of cultivating a strong brand image that aligns with our values and truth. We learned that our personal brand is not just about creating a façade or projecting an idealized version of ourselves. Instead, it is about being authentic and genuine, allowing our true selves to shine through in every interaction and representation. It is not necessary to have a massive online presence or celebrity status to cultivate a powerful personal brand. Instead, we discovered that a personal brand is a reflection of our values, expertise, and unique qualities, regardless of our public visibility.

We've ventured into the challenging terrain of crafting an online image that may not align with your true values and authenticity. The weight of this inauthenticity can slowly erode trust, hinder your progress, and even erect imposing barriers on your way to success. What we've highlighted is this: maintaining a seamless harmony between your personal brand and your true self is absolutely crucial. It's about ensuring that the online 'you' is a genuine reflection of the 'you' at your core.

By emphasizing the importance of maintaining consistency between our personal brand and our true selves, we can ensure that our reputation aligns with our overall vision and goals.

Our reputation precedes us, being the first thing that enters into rooms and shaping the way others perceive and engage with us. By nurturing a strong personal brand and upholding our values and truth, we create a positive reputation that opens doors, garners respect, and facilitates our progress towards our long-term vision.

The development of a personal brand within the context of the 15-year plan is a vital undertaking. It involves cultivating authenticity, aligning our image with our values, and understanding the significance of our reputation. Through building a personal brand that reflects our true selves, we set the stage for success, creating a solid foundation that supports our growth, fosters meaningful connections, and paves the way towards achieving our long-term vision.

CHAPTER 6: BULIDING YOUR NETWORK

The Essence Of Networking

Genuine opportunities flourish when we harness the dynamic force of collaboration. Collaborative efforts often lead to the discovery of new ideas, partnerships, and ventures that may not have been possible on our own. Being proactive to expand your network and nurturing connections with a diverse range of individuals, can expand our horizons and tap into a wealth of resources, knowledge, and support.

Effective networking goes beyond superficial interactions. Valuing each individual's unique contributions and actively seeking out meaningful connections, we create a network that offers valuable resources, support, and opportunities. Networking becomes a catalyst for personal and professional growth, fostering innovation, and enabling us to navigate the complexities of our industries with greater agility and success.

Networking serves as a powerful avenue to acquire diverse perspectives and insights that can elevate our professional growth. Engaging in conversations and interactions with our peers enables us to widen our comprehension of various industries, emerging trends, and optimal practices. This exposure to differing viewpoints encourages us to step beyond our own vantage point, compelling us to reevaluate our assumptions and expand our horizons. This, in turn, cultivates a richer well of creativity and innovation within our work and fosters more profound connections with those who engage with us.

None of this is not limited to formal events or professional settings. It extends to building connections and fostering relationships in various contexts, such as social gatherings, online communities, and industry-specific forums. Ensure you actively participate when you enter these spaces, as to create opportunities to connect with individuals from diverse backgrounds and expertise requires you to take steps forward not retreat. Top networkers are those that can actively engaging with others, listening attentively, and seek to build meaningful connections. It's about cultivating genuine relationships based on trust, respect, and shared interests.

In any given room or professional setting, it's important to understand that the most skilled individuals or those who appear to be decision-makers may not always be the sole source of valuable connections. When approaching networking with this mindset, one begins to appreciate that every individual has something unique to offer. It's about acknowledging that each person possesses valuable knowledge, experiences, and insights that can enrich our own understanding and open doors to new opportunities.

The Network Tier List

Just as it takes a village to raise a child, our ideas and goals are like our children that require the support and guidance of a strong network to flourish. The Network Tier List recognizes the power of collaboration and connection in nurturing our aspirations. Cultivate a diverse network, to create a village of individuals who can provide valuable insights, opportunities, and support. With their collective wisdom and resources, we can nurture and grow our ideas, bringing them to fruition within the context of the 15-year plan.

The philosophy behind this framework emphasizes the importance of tiering your contacts, understanding your position in their tiers, identifying potential networking goals & criteria, then developing a strategy that prioritizes high value networking.

The Network Tier List is based on the principle that not all contacts are created equal, people will always play the role they are best suited for. Some contacts are more influential, more well-connected, and more able to provide us with valuable opportunities than others. By identifying and ranking our contacts based on their level of influence, expertise, and ability to provide value, we can focus our networking efforts on those individuals who are most likely to help us achieve our goals.

The Tier List emphasizes the importance of reciprocity and mutual benefit in networking. You must recognize that networking is not just about what we can get from others, but also about what we can give. Being generous with our time, expertise, and resources, and looking for opportunities to help others in our network, can build strong relationships based on mutual trust and respect.

Another key aspect of this philosophy is the importance of setting clear networking goals and criteria. Identifying our specific networking goals and the criteria by which we will evaluate our contacts, ensures that our networking efforts are aligned with our overall goals and objectives.

Networking is an ongoing process that requires regular review and updating. Our networking goals and criteria may change over time, and our contacts may rise or fall in influence or relevance. Regularly review and update your tier list, to ensure that your networking efforts remain focused and effective. Ultimately, the Network Tier List is about taking ownership of our networking efforts and actively working to build a strong, high quality and supportive network of people who can help us achieve our goals.

Network Auditing

Network auditing involves a systematic examination of your connections. It's like taking stock of your assets. Identify the key individuals or groups in your network who can significantly contribute to your goals. The auditing process will uncover gaps in your network, enabling you to purposefully integrate individuals who could make valuable contributions. These connections, when combined, can form powerful clusters of resources and support. In the realm of networking, the upcoming 15 years will undoubtedly present instances where members of your network hold the potential to deliver remarkable benefits to your endeavours. However, it's vital to understand that networking transcends mere extraction of value from others; it equally pertains to what you can contribute.

Identify Your Networking Goals: Before you start building your network, it's important to identify your networking goals. These goals should align with your plan and the specific opportunities you are seeking. For example, if you want to become a CEO in the next 10 years, you might want to focus on building relationships with other executives and industry leaders.

Define Your Networking Criteria: To create your tier list, you need to define your networking criteria. This might include factors such as the person's level of influence, the quality of their network, their industry expertise, or their ability to provide you with valuable introductions or opportunities. The criteria may include things such as opportunities they bring, work ethic, personality traits in business, portfolio / credibility, a mutually beneficial approach, brokerage within their networks, adaptability / receptivity, vision in their own lives, independent thinker, expansive opportunities for personal growth, consistency / reliability.

Rank Your Network Contacts: Once you have your criteria in place, you can start ranking your network contacts. Assign each contact a ranking based on how well they meet your networking criteria. The tiered system helps you focus on those who are most influential or well-suited to aid in your objectives, recognizing that not every contact offers the same level of opportunity or insight.

Determine Your Networking Strategy Based On Your Tier List: You can develop a networking strategy that prioritizes your top-tier contacts. This might involve attending specific events or conferences where your top contacts will be present, reaching out to them for coffee or lunch, or offering to provide value to them in some way.

Regularly Review And Update Your Tier List: Your networking goals and criteria may change over time, so it's important to regularly review and update your tier list. Re-evaluate your network contacts based on their current level of influence, expertise, and ability to provide value to you.

To effectively place people into their appropriate networking tiers, it is essential to ask specific questions that assess their characteristics and the value they bring to your network. Consider the following questions Remember, these questions are designed to help you assess the different tiers within your network. It's important to evaluate each individual based on your relationship to them, their unique qualities, contributions, and potential for collaboration or support.

Tier 1 - Champions:

These are the top-tier individuals in your network who are instrumental in helping you achieve your goals. They are highly influential, well-respected, and well-connected in their respective fields. They bring significant opportunities, have strong work ethics, and exhibit positive personality traits in business. They have a strong portfolio and are highly credible. They are mutually beneficial, have expansive networks, and are highly adaptable and receptive to new ideas. They have a clear vision for their own lives and are always looking for opportunities for personal growth. They are highly consistent and reliable.

1. Who are the influential and well-connected individuals in my network?
2. Who has a strong portfolio and is highly credible in their field?
3. Who brings significant opportunities and has a positive impact on my goals?
4. Who exhibits strong work ethics and positive personality traits in business?
5. Who has a clear vision for their own lives and actively seeks personal growth?
6. Who is consistently reliable and adaptable to new ideas?

Tier 2 - Connectors:

These individuals have a wide network and are highly skilled at making introductions and connections. They may not have the same level of influence or opportunities as champions, but they are highly valuable because they can help you expand your network and connect you with other individuals who can help you achieve your goals.

1. Who are the individuals in my network who have a wide network of their own?
2. Who is skilled at making introductions and connections?
3. Who has a track record of connecting people to valuable opportunities?

4. Who can help me expand my network and connect with influential individuals?

Tier 3 - **Collaborators**:

Standing to your left and right, these individuals are highly skilled and knowledgeable in their respective fields, and they have a similar level of expertise as you do. They are valuable because they can provide you with advice, guidance, and support based on their own experiences.

1. Who are the individuals with a similar level of expertise and knowledge in my field?
2. Who can provide valuable advice, guidance, and support based on their experiences?
3. Who has a willingness to collaborate and work together on projects or initiatives?
4. Who can contribute to my professional growth through mutual learning and sharing?

Tier 4 - **Enthusiasts**:

These individuals are passionate and dedicated learners who actively seek to expand their knowledge and skills in their respective fields. While they may not have the same level of expertise or opportunities as the other tiers, they are highly motivated to collaborate and contribute to the network. Enthusiasts bring value through their eagerness to learn from others, their willingness to engage in meaningful discussions, and their openness to sharing insights and perspectives. They actively seek mentorship and guidance from the higher tiers while bringing a fresh perspective and a hunger for growth to the network.

1. Who are the passionate learners in my network who actively seek knowledge and growth?
2. Who has a hunger for collaborating, contributing, and sharing insights?
3. Who actively seeks mentorship and guidance from higher-tier individuals?

4. Who brings a fresh perspective and eagerness to learn and engage in meaningful discussions?

Tier 5 - Supporters:

These individuals are highly supportive and encouraging, and they may not have the same level of expertise or opportunities as champions or collaborators. However, they are highly valuable because they provide emotional support and encouragement, which is essential for long-term success.

1. Who are the individuals in my network who provide emotional support and encouragement?
2. Who consistently uplifts and motivates me on my journey towards success?
3. Who may not have the same level of expertise but play a crucial role in my long-term success?

Tier 6 - Peripheral contacts:

These are individuals who are in your network but do not have a direct impact on your goals or success. While they may not be as valuable as the other tiers, it is still important to maintain positive relationships with them, as they can still provide some value and may become more valuable in the future.

1. Who are the individuals in my network who may not have a direct impact on my goals?
2. Who are the acquaintances or connections that I maintain positive relationships with?
3. Who may still provide some value or have the potential to become more valuable in the future?

Tier Movement:

As we progress on our journey, we must acknowledge that change is a constant factor. Over time, various factors will influence the roles our network connections play in our lives. Like the shifting seasons, our network's dynamics evolve. Tier movement is the exploration of how individuals in our network transition between tiers based on their changing roles, contributions, and our evolving goals. Let's explore this dynamic aspect of networking for practical insights into our continued growth and success

- ❖ Have any individuals in higher tiers shown a decreased level of engagement or relevance to my current goals?
- ❖ Are there contacts in lower tiers who have recently demonstrated a strong commitment to my objectives and could be considered for promotion?
- ❖ Can I identify instances where someone's skills or resources have evolved, making them better suited for a higher tier?
- ❖ Have any individuals in my network taken on new roles or responsibilities that may warrant a change in their tier placement?
- ❖ Are there any collaborations or interactions that suggest certain contacts should be reevaluated for tier placement?
- ❖ Have I encountered individuals who consistently provide valuable insights or opportunities but may be in a lower tier?
- ❖ Have any changes in my goals or aspirations influenced the relevance of specific contacts within my network tiers?
- ❖ Can I identify individuals whose contributions align more closely with a different tier based on recent interactions or developments?

Pro Tip: The Perception Puzzle - Shaping Your Image In Other Networks

In the vast and intricate web of personal networks, your placement and reputation are not fixed entities, but dynamic constructs influenced by interactions and individual perspectives. Imagine each person's mind as a canvas, where you paint a unique portrait of yourself through your words, actions, and demeanour. Understand that you embody different roles and diverse identities in the minds of those around you, influenced by their experiences, perceptions, and the impressions you leave behind.

Like a master artist, you have the power to craft these perceptions deliberately, moulding your image to align with your aspirations and goals. Start by cultivating self-awareness and understanding how you come across to others. Reflect on your values, strengths, and areas for improvement, seeking to project an authentic version of yourself that resonates with your true essence.

Every encounter is an opportunity to create a masterpiece. Approach each interaction with intention and purpose, imbuing it with authenticity, empathy, and respect. Be fully present, listening attentively and engaging genuinely, leaving an indelible mark that captures the essence of your character and resonates with the hearts and minds of others.

Embrace the power of storytelling to shape your narrative in others' networks. Share compelling stories that highlight your journey, lessons learned, and moments of triumph and growth. Craft narratives that resonate with others, touching their hearts and sparking connections. Authenticity is key—be genuine, vulnerable, and willing to share both successes and failures, allowing others to relate to your experiences and feel a sense of camaraderie.

Remember that perceptions are not solely shaped by your actions but also influenced by how others interpret and filter the information they receive. Acknowledge that you cannot control others' perspectives entirely, you possess the ability to influence them through consistent behaviour, meaningful contributions, and a reputation built on trust and reliability. Be mindful of your digital footprint, for the online realm amplifies the impact of your words and deeds. Craft a personal brand that aligns with your values, projecting an image that embodies your true essence.

In the dynamic landscape of personal networks, where impressions are malleable and perceptions evolve, you have the opportunity to shape how others view you. Embrace this power, approach each interaction as an artistic expression, and paint a vivid portrait of yourself that inspires trust, fosters connections, and aligns with your long-term vision. By cultivating self-awareness, engaging authentically, and crafting compelling narratives, you can enhance your placement in others' networks and nurture meaningful relationships that support your growth and success throughout your journey.

Characters In Your Network

The power of networking has become more evident than ever. Building a strong and diverse network of individuals can significantly impact your personal and professional journey. Why is it essential to have different types of people in your network? The answer lies in the unique perspectives, opportunities, and support they can offer.

The Coach: A Coach is an invaluable asset in a strong personal network, providing guidance, advice, and support based on their expertise and experience. They share their knowledge, offer practical insights, and help navigate challenges, accelerating personal and professional growth. Having a Coach ensures access to a trusted advisor who contributes significantly to ongoing development and success.

The Industry Insider: The Industry Insider is a crucial component of a strong personal network, particularly for those aiming to excel in a specific industry. With extensive knowledge, expertise, and a wide network, they provide valuable opportunities, guidance, and a competitive edge. Their deep understanding of industry trends and connections with influential individuals offer insights into best practices, access to new opportunities, and mentorship, empowering you to thrive in your chosen field. Leveraging the Industry Insider's expertise and network enhances your industry knowledge and enables effective navigation within your professional sphere.

The Trendsetter: The Trendsetter is a valuable asset in a strong personal network, especially for individuals striving to stay ahead in their industry. With their ability to identify emerging trends, innovative thinking, and valuable insights, they provide a competitive edge. The Trendsetter's forward-thinking mindset allows them to anticipate and adapt to changing dynamics, while their creative spirit drives them to explore new ideas and challenge norms. Engaging with the Trendsetter inspires you to think differently, embrace innovation, and pursue unconventional solutions.

The Connector: The Connector in your personal network is an invaluable asset, possessing a unique talent for building relationships and connecting people. They excel at identifying synergies and facilitating meaningful connections, leveraging their extensive network spanning various industries and backgrounds. Engaging with the Connector opens doors to new opportunities, collaborations, and partnerships, expanding your own network and gaining access to valuable resources.

The Realist: The Realist in your personal network brings a practical perspective and grounded advice to navigate challenges realistically. Engaging with them helps you make informed decisions, assess opportunities and risks objectively, and gain practical insights based on their experiences. Their guidance saves time and effort by helping you avoid common pitfalls and take a more efficient path towards your goals. Embrace the value of having a Realist in your network, setting realistic goals, and making informed decisions for increased chances of success.

The Visionary: The Visionary in your personal network possesses the ability to think long-term, challenge conventional thinking, and offer strategic insights and foresight. Engaging with them expands your thinking, inspires you to pursue ambitious goals, and breaks free from limiting beliefs. They provide a strategic perspective, anticipate trends, and guide you towards meaningful outcomes. Embrace the transformative power of having a Visionary in your network, aligning your goals with a larger vision, and leveraging their insights for a competitive advantage.

The Partner: The Partner in your personal network is a trusted collaborator who shares your goals and values. They provide support, accountability, and collaboration opportunities, contributing to your growth and success. Engaging with them fosters a strong partnership based on mutual support and encouragement. They offer practical assistance, feedback, and resources, instilling confidence and keeping you focused. The synergy created by working together leads to innovative solutions and increased productivity. Embrace the value of having a Partner in your network, leveraging their support and collaboration to achieve shared goals.

The Dreamers: The Dreamers are ambitious individuals in your network who inspire and challenge you to reach new heights. Their unwavering determination and willingness to take risks push you beyond your limits. Engaging with them creates a supportive alliance where you exchange ideas, strategies, and resources. Their stories of resilience and growth provide valuable lessons and inspiration. Embrace the influence of the Dreamers to propel yourself towards your own dreams.

Remember, the key is to build a diverse network with individuals who bring different perspectives, expertise, and support to your personal and professional journey.

Chapter Summary

We have delved into the depths of human connections and unveil the concept of the Network Tier List as a guiding compass for achieving our long-term aspirations.

Through thought-provoking insights, we explore how our network influences our identity and shapes our trajectory towards success. By consciously curating our connections, we can craft a supportive ecosystem that propels us forward on our path. Drawing from the depths of human perception, we unveil the lens that paints your picture in the eyes of others; people see us differently based on their unique perspectives and interactions. This revelation empowers us to wield our influence effectively and make each interaction as masterpiece. Understanding the impact, we have on others and how we can harness it to our advantage in the pursuit of our long-term goals.

Central to our exploration is the dynamic nature of the Network Tier List. As our relationships evolve over the 15-year span, this framework serves as an invaluable tool for understanding, organizing, and nurturing our connections. It allows us to filter and prioritize individuals who align with our long-term vision, ensuring that our network remains relevant, robust, and capable of fuelling our aspirations.

By curating our connections, understanding their perception of us, approaching networking purposefully, embracing reciprocity, and utilizing the Network Tier List as our steadfast guide, we can forge alliances that align with our plans, amplifying our growth and achievements along the way.

CHAPTER 7: EFFECTIVE CONVERSATIONS MASTERY

Effective Conversations Mastery

Imagine a world where daunting discussions become gateways to understanding, where differences become bridges, and where conflicts evolve into collaborative resolutions. With this framework, you are embarking on a journey that will empower you to not only navigate these complexities with finesse but to emerge from them as a more adept communicator, a more empathetic listener, and a more resilient individual.

Through practical techniques, and actionable steps, this framework is designed to be a dynamic tool that adapts to various contexts, whether personal, professional, or social. After mastering these pillars, you'll not only enhance your communication skills but also cultivate deeper connections, promote understanding, and unravel the true potential of every conversation.

Unveiling the Hidden Gems Within Difficult Conversations.

Each conversation, regardless of its nature, offers a chance for learning and progression. Yet, it is the arduous and uncomfortable dialogues that provide the richest soil for personal evolution. We often will feel the discomfort physically, making us turn away and retreating with silence or avoidance of the issue, but this should be the exact signal we take, to push through. Difficult discussions compel us to confront our biases, question assumptions, and broaden our horizons. They are an arena for honing communication skills, emotional intelligence, and conflict resolution prowess. Recognizing difficult conversations as gateways to self-improvement, we seamlessly transform what might initially appear as barriers into steppingstones toward a refined version of ourselves.

To navigate intricate conversations with finesse, we require a well-structured mental approach, equipped with the frameworks and strategies that empower constructive and confident engagement. Our overarching objective within these pages is to furnish individuals with tools, endowing them with the ability to adeptly manage a diverse array of challenging dialogues. Use this framework as a map to carve a path through the labyrinthine of emotions, diverse perspectives, and potential conflicts inherent to such conversations.

Your aim isn't merely to survive these encounters but to emerge from them with fresh insights, fortified connections, and an elevated capacity to navigate future trials. Rather than regarding challenging conversations as obstacles, we perceive them as vehicles propelling our personal evolution. Embrace these exchanges and you will unlock a reservoir of potential that propels us toward heightened self-awareness, resilience, and mastery in the art of effective communication.

The Four Pillars: Context, Emotion, Perspective, Resolution

The core of impactful conversations is anchored in The Four Pillars: Context, Emotion, Perspective, and Resolution, which serve as guides through the complexities of dialogue. The framework identifies and encapsulates the foundational elements present in every exchange, regardless of its topic or nature. Breaking down the landscape of conversation into these four essential aspects brings clarity and purpose to our interactions, revealing the path forward with deeper insight and intentionality.

1. **Context**: This cornerstone solidifies the foundation by underscoring the pivotal role of comprehending the context within which a conversation unfolds. Context serves as the canvas on which words are painted and actions are sculpted. It enfolds the setting, historical backdrop, pertinent information, and relevant circumstances that contribute to the conversation's essence and objective.
2. **Emotion:** Emotion forms an integral tapestry within human communication. Acknowledging and addressing emotions serves as a linchpin in forging connections and nurturing understanding. This pillar accentuates the significance of emotional intelligence – the acumen to recognize, apprehend, and manage both our own and others' emotions. Acknowledging emotions and their impact is a key factor to navigating conversations with empathy.
3. **Perspective**: Each dialogue brims with manifold viewpoints and angles. This pillar highlights the importance of active listening and empathy in apprehending these diverse outlooks. By refining the art of empathetic engagement, we bridge chasms in understanding and foster an environment where mutual respect and receptivity flourish.

4. **Resolution**: Ultimately, the crux of many conversations lies in attaining resolution or common ground. This pillar underscores the weight of nurturing collaborative resolution strategies. It impels individuals to collaborate in uncovering solutions, recalibrating discussions for clarity, and pursuing compromises that align with the collective objectives of the discourse.

The essence of The Four Pillars lies in its simplicity and universality. It isn't shackled to specific discourse types or themes – rather, it presents an adaptable scaffold applicable to dialogues spanning personal, professional, and social terrains. Whether negotiating a business transaction, reconciling a conflict with a loved one, or participating in a community dialogue, these pillars retain their relevance.

The framework takes conversations from intricate dialogues and tapestries of experiences, into manageable constituents that can be dissected, comprehended, and navigated with enhanced effectiveness.

Context: The Keystone Of Understanding

Words on their own aren't inherently good or bad, context is what gives their true meaning. Context constitutes the bedrock upon which effective communication stands. Acknowledging context's sway makes us recognize that two individuals may construe the same words or actions differently, owing to their unique experiences and perspectives. Comprehending context empowers us to engage in conversations with empathy and receptiveness. It prompts us to factor in the array of variables shaping another's perspective, affording us insight into the intricate tapestry of human thought.

Discern Facts from Assumptions, Cultivating Balanced Insight

Distinguishing facts from assumptions is a critical aptitude in effective communication. Assumptions often sprout from incomplete information, biases, or preconceived notions, fostering misunderstandings and misinterpretations. Interrogate your assumptions, ask high quality questions to find factual foundations before drawing conclusions and ultimately discover the broader context informing someone's expressions or deeds.

Separating factual points from assumptions fosters a balance in our comprehension of information. This practice nurtures an environment where conversations are anchored in accuracy rather than misconceptions. It also champions humility, as we concede that our initial assumptions may not always mirror reality.

When both parties in a conversation hold an understanding of the contextual backdrop framing the discussion, they can participate more productively, appreciating one another's vantage points and collaborating to pinpoint common ground.

Emotion Intelligence: Guiding Your Emotional Navigation

Emotions like subtle currents, shape the course of every conversation, molding its tone, coloring our responses, and ultimate outcomes for situations. Emotions are not solely abstract concepts; they also have strong physiological underpinnings. When encountering difficult situations, our nervous system activates the "fight or flight" response, releasing stress hormones like cortisol, which can affect our functions and influence emotional responses.

This phase of the "E.C.M.F" delves into the profound realm of emotional intelligence, casting light upon its pivotal role in skillfully navigating challenging conversations with grace and empathy.

Elevate Emotional Awareness For Smoother Conversations

At the foundation of emotional intelligence lies emotional awareness. By recognizing and acknowledging both our own emotions and those of others, we lay the groundwork for authenticity and vulnerability.

Elevating emotional awareness involves tuning into the nuanced shifts in mood, body language, and intonation – signals that unveil the concealed emotions beneath the surface. This heightened awareness serves to prevent misunderstandings and paves the way for constructive emotional address.

When emotions find recognition, individuals experience validation and a sense of being heard, thus nurturing more harmonious and respectful conversations. We must tune our emotional sensors to be able to pick up on these shifts in conversation; adjust your pace, take a moment between speaking, let the energy settle in the discussion before rushing ahead and reacting. If a storm is raging around you, do not leave your sails open to be carried in a direction not of your own making, reduce your speed to make it easier to navigate through rough waters until you are ready to unfurl and flow again.

Mastery Over Personal Emotions

Left unchecked, emotions can surge and thwart productive communication. Cultivating emotional regulation empowers us to approach conversations from a place of equanimity and thoughtfulness, regardless of the intensity of the subject matter.

The brain's structure allows us to reshape its neural pathways over time through intentional, consistent actions. Seek to build a regular practice for increasing emotional regulation, such as deep breathing exercises or meditation to promote calmer responses to challenging emotions.

Rewiring our responses allows us to tame our own emotions, carve out space for empathy and increasing consciousness of its responses, leaves us better equipped to forge genuine connections with others. Engage in techniques that promote mental change, such as mindfulness and gradual exposure, while incorporating a daily practice to affirm the new mental responses you are developing. Connecting the mental and physical will allow you to bond better and have trust nurtured, paving the way for more profound and meaningful exchanges.

Exploring Perspectives: Empathy As The Bridge

The multitude of human experiences and viewpoints is both a source of opulence and a potential catalyst for misunderstanding and discord. Empathy is a mighty force that humanizes interactions. It empowers us to transcend disparities, even amidst disagreement, in pursuit of common ground. By earnestly seeking to understand the diverse perspectives of others, we unlock a realm of insight and connection. You must walk a mile in others' shoes, to truly fathom and feel their experiences, but with empathy we can at least feel their perspective and build a connection.

In conversations, it's insufficient to merely hear words; active listening is essential to understanding the emotions, convictions, and life experiences that underpin those words. Empathetic listening entails putting aside our own judgments and preconceived notions, genuinely comprehending where the other person is coming from.

Embracing this form of communication permits us to traverse the waves of emotions brought on by tough conversations adeptly, through recognizing and validating feelings without judgment. It serves to de-escalate tense situations, as individuals feel understood and acknowledged, thus cultivating an environment ripe for constructive dialogue. Actively listen, formulate open-ended questions, and responding with authentic compassion, when looking to communicate with another person.

Pro Tip: The Significance Of Active Listening

Active listening stands as a quintessential skill in effective communication. It entails dedicating full attention to the speaker – not merely their words, but also their emotions, body language, and intentions. By practicing active listening, we forge an environment where people feel heard.

Active listening is the bedrock of empathy. Through it, we showcase our commitment to understanding and honoring the speaker's viewpoint. This establishes trust and ushers in candid and honest dialogue, even when tackling sensitive or contentious issues.

Implementing The "Empathy Bridge" To Bridge Perspective Gaps

The "Empathy Bridge" technique is a practical tool for constructing connections through empathy. It entails a deliberate endeavor to apprehend not only the spoken words, but also the emotions and experiences underlying them. Pose probing questions, reflect upon the conveyed content, and acknowledging the emotions at play, to construct a bridge that traverses the void between viewpoints.

Three Levels Of Constructing An Empathy Bridge

1. **Attentive Connection:** Begin by cultivating an attentive presence. Eliminate distractions and fully focus on the speaker. Engage in active listening to comprehend both spoken words and non-verbal cues. This level sets the foundation for empathetic understanding.
2. **Reflective Engagement:** Practice reflective validation to confirm your understanding. Acknowledge the emotions expressed by the speaker, naming them to create emotional resonance. Seek common ground or shared experiences to build rapport. Express your understanding and commitment to mutual empathy.
3. **Open Dialogue And Learning:** Nurture open dialogue by maintaining a non-judgmental stance. Allow the conversation to unfold naturally, giving the speaker ample time to share without interruptions. Afterward, reflect on the interaction to enhance your empathetic capacity and enrich future connections.

Incorporating these three levels—attentive connection, reflective engagement, and open dialogue— creates a structured approach to building empathy bridges, fostering deeper connections and bridging perspective gaps with authenticity and empathy.

Resolution: Navigating Toward Shared Ground

Effective conversations extend beyond understanding and empathy; they culminate in a clear path toward resolution. In this section of the Effective Conversations Mastery Framework, (E.C.M.F) we delve into strategies guiding conversations toward collaborative resolutions, transforming challenges into gateways for growth and shared comprehension.

Exploring Strategies For Collaborative Resolution in Complex Conversations

Complex conversations often arise from divergent viewpoints, conflicting interests, or entrenched positions. Successfully navigating these conversations necessitates strategies emphasizing collaboration and compromise.

Collaborative resolution strategies entail seeking win-win outcomes where all parties feel valued and content with the result.

These strategies pivot the mindset from adversarial to cooperative, entailing recognition of shared objectives, identification of commonalities, and brainstorming of creative solutions that respect everyone's needs.

The Art Of Reframing For Clarity And Alignment

The framing of a conversation significantly influences its trajectory. Reframing involves shifting the focus or perspective of the dialogue to uncover shared ground or highlight common interests. This technique defuses tension and enables participants to view the situation from a fresh vantage point. By reframing discussions, we prompt participants to explore alternative viewpoints and contemplate potential solutions that might not have been evident initially. This cultivates a space for innovative thought and unveils new pathways for resolution.

Ask yourself targeted questions to create an opportunity to unearth shared values and objectives, transcending initial barriers and fostering deeper understanding.

Key Questions For Effective Reframing:

- ❖ **What Assumptions Am I Making?** Probe into your underlying assumptions to uncover biases that might influence your perspective.
- ❖ **How Might Others Perceive This?** Step into the shoes of others involved to gain insights into their viewpoints and motivations.
- ❖ **What Shared Objectives Exist?** Identify common goals or interests that can shift the focus towards collaborative solutions.
- ❖ **What New Insights Can I Uncover?** Challenge yourself to explore unconventional angles to gain fresh insights.
- ❖ **How Can We Reframe the Narrative?** Craft language that fosters collaboration and mutual understanding instead of perpetuating conflicts.
- ❖ **What Is The Bigger Picture?** Zoom out to consider the larger context. Reflect on how the current conversation fits within broader goals, overarching values, and future implications.

The Effective Conversations Mastery Framework offers a transformative journey, equipping individuals with the tools to navigate intricate conversations with finesse and emerge as adept communicators. Through its Four Pillars— Context, Emotion, Perspective, and Resolution—this framework enables a profound understanding of dialogue complexities. It champions emotional intelligence and empathetic listening, fostering connections and mutual understanding.

The framework empowers the navigation of challenges toward growth and shared comprehension, so embracing collaborative resolution strategies and the art of reframing it empowers individuals to unlock the potential of every conversation, fostering resilience, empathy, and effective communication across personal, professional, and social contexts.

Chapter Summary

We have acquired the skills of high-level communicators, capable of turning challenging conversations into opportunities for growth and connection. We began by understanding that conversations are gateways to understanding, and differences can serve as bridges to connection, offering us a path to personal growth. This framework equips us with the tools needed for adaptive communication in various aspects of our lives.

The first pillar, Context, taught us the importance of understanding the backdrop of our conversations. Distinguishing facts from assumptions helps us gain a balanced perspective, facilitating accurate comprehension. This skill is essential for building strong foundations in any dialogue.

Moving on to the second pillar, Emotion, we explored the significance of emotional intelligence. By understanding the physiological basis of emotions and practicing emotional regulation, we can navigate challenging conversations with grace and thoughtfulness. The "Empathy Bridge" technique showed us how to step into others' worlds authentically, enhancing our ability to connect.

The third pillar, Perspective, emphasized the richness of diverse viewpoints. Through active listening and empathy, we learned how to create meaningful connections, even when faced with disagreements. Building empathy bridges became a key strategy for forging deeper connections and mutual understanding.

Finally, the fourth pillar, Resolution, guided us towards collaborative solutions in complex conversations. By shifting our mindset from adversarial to cooperative, we explored techniques like reframing to discover common ground and innovative solutions.

The Effective Conversations Mastery Framework empowers us to navigate the complexities of communication with finesse. Through emotional intelligence and empathetic listening, we can foster connections. Collaborative resolution strategies and the art of reframing equip us to address challenges, promoting resilience and effective communication across various contexts.

In essence, this chapter has illuminated the transformative power of conversations. It has enabled us to become adept communicators who embrace differences and find common ground. By mastering these principles, we can navigate the intricacies of dialogue with grace, empathy, and a deep understanding of the human experience.

CHAPTER 8:
NAVIGATING SETBACKS

Continuous Improvement

Once you've meticulously crafted your plan, set your goals, and charted your course for the future, the real work begins. It is in the daily grind and the unwavering commitment to continuous improvement that individuals and organizations propel themselves towards their desired destination. Continuous improvement is not a static endpoint; it is an ongoing journey that embraces excellence, growth, and innovation throughout a lifetime.

At the heart of continuous improvement lies a commitment to excellence. It is a dedication to setting high standards, pursuing quality in every aspect of work, and continuously seeking ways to enhance performance. This unwavering pursuit of perfection, even knowing it may be elusive, becomes the guiding principle that infuses every action and decision.

However, continuous improvement does not flourish in isolation. It thrives in an environment that fosters collaboration, open communication, and innovation. It is through this ongoing journey of continuous improvement that individuals and organizations can realize their long-term vision and achieve sustainable success within the framework of the 15-year plan. It is the unwavering commitment to excellence, the reliance on data-driven decision-making, and the cultivation of a collaborative and innovative culture that propel them forward, bringing them ever closer to their desired destination.

As they navigate this journey, they continuously refine their practices, optimize their performance, and seize opportunities for learning and development.

The Art Of Continuous Self-Updating

In an era defined by continuous technological advancements and ever-evolving innovation, the concept of updating and upgrading has woven itself into the fabric of our lives. We eagerly await the release of cutting-edge gadgets, invest time in enhancing our devices for peak performance, and enthusiastically embrace the latest trends in fashion, lifestyle, and beyond. Yet, within this whirlwind of external progress, a crucial aspect often remains neglected: our personal growth and evolution.

The Dichotomy Of Stagnation

In our pursuit of bettering our material possessions, a paradox emerges. We dedicate substantial resources and energy to enhance our material lives while inadvertently overlooking the very core that empowers us to navigate this dynamic landscape: our personal development. Picture a scenario where you possess state-of-the-art gadgets and a high-tech vehicle, yet your skills and knowledge remain unchanged. This paradox underscores the profound gap between external acquisitions and the intrinsic enrichment that propels our journey. A tool is only as good as the person using it.

The Three Pillars Of Self-Updating: Mindset, Skills, And Knowledge

1. **Mindset:** Our mindset functions as the compass guiding our thoughts, decisions, and actions. Embracing a growth mindset—one that welcomes challenges and views failures as steppingstones to improvement—is pivotal in the journey of self-updating. Conversely, a fixed mindset can lead to complacency and hinder personal progress. Cultivating a growth-oriented mindset involves nurturing self-awareness, practicing self-compassion, and embracing change to adapt to new situations.

2. **Skills**: Just as software necessitates regular updates for optimal functionality, our skills demand ongoing attention. Nurturing skills is essential for navigating the complexities of our ever-changing world. Whether it involves mastering a programming language, refining communication prowess, or honing a creative craft, fostering skills is paramount. Self-updating skills entails recognizing growth opportunities, setting explicit goals, and unwaveringly committing to elevate our abilities.

3. **Knowledge**: The digital age has bestowed upon us a vast reservoir of knowledge at our fingertips. Yet, amidst this abundance, lies the

challenge of discernment. Self-updating knowledge involves consciously selecting pertinent and valuable information that aligns with our individual and professional ambitions. Regular reading, exposure to diverse sources, and seeking fresh perspectives contribute to a well-rounded and informed knowledge base.

Embracing Intentionality: Depth Over Breadth

In a culture often valuing perpetual activity, the concept that quality triumphs over quantity can fade into the background. Self-updating isn't a race to accumulate numerous skills, saturate our minds with data, or hastily align with every trend. Instead, it signifies a deliberate choice to prioritize depth over breadth. Ensure to emphasize quality, to ensure that cultivated skills are not merely acquired but mastered, the mindset nurtured isn't just resilient but robust, and the knowledge gained isn't just abundant but profound and practically applicable.

Failing Successfully

In the pursuit of our long-term goals, we often focus on success and the achievement of our objectives. However, amidst our journey, it is crucial to acknowledge that failure is an inevitable part of the process. Rather than viewing failure as a roadblock, we can learn to embrace it as a valuable teacher and catalyst for growth. Understanding that failure is often a natural and necessary part of any significant endeavours enables individuals to maintain resilience and perseverance when faced with obstacles.

Perceiving failure as a valuable learning experience opens the door to extracting lessons and insights from each setback. Failure provides an opportunity to reflect upon the decisions, strategies, or circumstances that contributed to the outcome. By examining these factors, individuals can identify areas for improvement, refine their approaches, and develop a more informed understanding of their strengths and weaknesses.

The Power Of Perspective

Perspective is the lens through which we view the world and interpret our experiences. It shapes our understanding, influences our emotions, and guides our actions. Our perspective can be empowering or limiting, constructive or destructive, depending on the lenses we choose to wear. Lenses are the filters that colour our perception, shaping how we interpret events and situations.

They can be positive, helping us see opportunities, learn from setbacks, and maintain a growth mindset. On the other hand, lenses can also be negative, clouding our judgment, fostering self-doubt, and inhibiting our potential. By cultivating awareness of our lenses and actively choosing the ones that serve us best, we can shape our perspective in a way that empowers us. Embracing a positive lens allows us to see failure as a temporary setback or a valuable learning experience.

Ultimately, our perspective and the lenses we choose have a profound impact on how we navigate the world, respond to failure, and pursue our long-term goals.

Shaping The Image Of Failure

The Lens Of Temporary Setback: Rather than viewing failure as a permanent endpoint, recognize it as a temporary setback. Understand that setbacks are not permanent roadblocks but temporary detours on the path to success. This perspective allows for resilience and perseverance in the face of obstacles.

The Lens Of Learning Experience: Embrace failure as a valuable learning experience. See it as an opportunity to reflect on decisions, strategies, and circumstances that contributed to the outcome. Extract lessons and insights from each setback to identify areas for improvement, refine approaches, and gain a deeper understanding of strengths and weaknesses.

The Lens Of Growth Mindset: Adopt a growth mindset that sees failure as an opportunity for growth and improvement. Cultivate optimism

121

and possibility by embracing challenges as learning experiences. This mindset shift fosters creativity, innovation, and a willingness to take risks, as individuals are open to exploring new territories and pushing their boundaries.

By adopting these perspectives, individuals can reshape their image of failure. Failure becomes a steppingstone toward success, a temporary setback that offers valuable lessons and growth opportunities. This shift in perspective enables individuals to maintain resilience, extract insights, and cultivate a mindset that embraces challenges and sees failure as a catalyst for personal and professional development.

Negative Lenses That Can Colour The Image Of Failure

The Lens Of Self-Doubt: Doubting one's abilities and worth based on failure can hinder progress and limit future opportunities. Overcoming self-doubt involves cultivating self-belief, practicing self-compassion, and embracing a growth mindset that recognizes failures as opportunities for learning and improvement.

The Lens Of Blame: Placing blame solely on external factors or others for failures avoids personal responsibility and inhibits learning from mistakes. Taking ownership of failures and reflecting on one's actions and decisions allows for personal growth, resilience, and the development of effective problem-solving skills.

The Lens Of Perfectionism: Striving for perfection and expecting flawless outcomes sets unrealistic expectations and creates unnecessary pressure. Embracing a mindset that values progress over perfection allows for a healthier perspective on failure, promoting resilience, adaptability, and continuous improvement.

The Lens Of A Fixed Mindset: Believing that intelligence and abilities are fixed traits limits growth and hinders the willingness to take risks. Embracing a growth mindset fosters a belief in the potential for development and encourages resilience in the face of failures, leading to a willingness to learn, adapt, and overcome challenges.

The Lens Of Catastrophizing: Magnifying failures and perceiving them as catastrophic events can paralyze progress and deter future attempts. Cultivating resilience involves reframing failures as temporary setbacks, focusing on solutions rather than dwelling on problems, and maintaining a positive outlook to build the confidence needed to persevere.

Recognizing these negative lenses is crucial for overcoming their influence and adopting a more positive and constructive perspective towards failure. By challenging these negative perspectives, individuals can embrace a growth mindset, take personal responsibility, and view failure as a valuable learning experience.

Perception Of Competition

Competition is a powerful driver for personal growth, but its impact greatly depends on the choices we make regarding our surroundings. Understanding how to choose the right opponents, embrace setbacks as opportunities, harness competition as motivation, and cultivate a growth mindset, individuals can create a framework for limitless personal development.

Competition serves as a powerful motivational force, igniting drive and ambition. It fuels innovation, progress, and self-discipline. The room we choose to operate in can either propel our growth or confine us within a limited capacity. Selecting opponents who inspire and challenge us is crucial. Rather than seeking weaker adversaries, we should surround ourselves with individuals who possess admirable qualities, skills, and work ethics. Their presence will motivate us to push beyond our limits and strive for excellence.

Healthy competition is a catalyst for personal growth. By choosing the right opponents, embracing losses as learning experiences, harnessing competition as a motivational force, and nurturing a growth mindset, individuals unlock their potential and achieve excellence. Competition pushes individuals to their limits, fosters innovation, and develops resilience. With the right mindset, individuals can maximize their growth and success through the power of healthy competition.

Extracting Lessons From Failure

When faced with failure, it is important to recognize that each setback carries valuable lessons that can profoundly shape our future actions. Taking the time to reflect on the reasons behind the failure is a crucial step in the process of failing successfully within a 15-year timeline. Instead of dwelling on the negative aspects of failure, individuals can reframe it as a steppingstone towards success. Every failure carries valuable lessons that can shape our future actions.

Questions To Ask Yourself:

- ❖ What were my initial expectations and goals?
- ❖ What specific actions did I take to achieve those goals?
- ❖ What were the key factors that contributed to the failure?
- ❖ Were there any external factors beyond my control?
- ❖ Did I adequately assess and manage risks?
- ❖ Did I seek advice or guidance from others? E.g., Were there any warning signs or red flags that I ignored?
- ❖ Did I effectively communicate and collaborate with others?
- ❖ Did I allocate resources appropriately?
- ❖ What were the primary obstacles or challenges I encountered?

Breaking Down The Information:

Identify The Root Causes: Analyse the contributing factors and identify the underlying root causes of the failure.
Categorize The Lessons: Group the lessons learned into specific categories such as decision-making, communication, planning, resource management, risk assessment, or collaboration.

Prioritize Key Insights: Determine the most significant and actionable lessons that have the potential to create the greatest impact on future endeavours.

Create An Action Plan: Break down the lessons into actionable steps and strategies to implement moving forward.

Reflect On Personal Growth: Consider how the failure has contributed to personal growth, resilience, and learning experiences.

Achieving Breakthroughs:

Importance And Impact: Assess the significance and potential impact of each lesson learned on future decision-making and goal attainment.

Depth Of Understanding: Evaluate the depth of understanding achieved through the reflection process and the insights gained from self-analysis.

Emotional Resonance: Consider the emotional resonance and personal significance of each breakthrough in terms of self-awareness, mindset shifts, or behaviour changes.

Practical Applicability: Evaluate the practical applicability of the mental breakthroughs in real-life scenarios and their potential to drive positive change.

These lessons serve as guideposts for future endeavours, helping individuals refine their approach and strengthen their future endeavours. Through deep understanding of the shortcomings and pitfalls that led to failure, individuals can make more informed decisions, develop more effective strategies, and avoid repeating past mistakes. This mindset fosters innovation, resilience, and adaptability, enabling individuals to make continuous progress towards their long-term goals.

Resilience And Perseverance

Resilience is the ability to recover quickly from setbacks, adversity, and failure. It involves developing a mindset that allows individuals to navigate through challenging circumstances with strength and determination. Cultivating resilience requires acknowledging that setbacks and failures are normal and expected on the path to success. Instead of being discouraged or disheartened by failure, individuals with resilience see it as an opportunity to learn, grow, and improve.

When faced with failure, individuals with resilience take the time to reflect on what went wrong and seek lessons from the experience. They do not let failure define them but instead use it as fuel for personal and professional growth. Taking time to analyse the factors that contributed to the failure, individuals can adjust their strategies, make necessary course corrections, and develop new approaches that are more likely to lead to success.

Perseverance is another key component of failing successfully within a 15-year timeline. It is the ability to stay committed and determined in the face of challenges and setbacks. Perseverance involves maintaining a long-term perspective and not allowing temporary failures to derail progress. Individuals who persevere understand that setbacks are not permanent, that success often requires sustained effort and resilience.

To develop a resilient mindset and perseverance, individuals can adopt several strategies. They can cultivate a positive attitude and optimism, focusing on the potential for growth and improvement rather than dwelling on the setbacks. Setting realistic expectations and understanding that progress may be nonlinear can also help maintain motivation during challenging times.

Understand that setbacks and failures are part of the journey towards long-term success allows a person to maintain emotional stability in turbulent times. The most successful achievers cultivate the ability to bounce back from failures, learning from them and adapting your strategies accordingly. Develop a resilient mindset that allows you to persevere, stay motivated, and maintain focus on your long term goals, despite encountering obstacles along the way.

Pivoting Successfully

A pivot involves making a significant shift in your goals, plans, or direction to better align with your evolving aspirations or to respond to external factors. One of the key benefits of these frameworks lay in their flexibility. While it provides a roadmap for your long-term goals, it also acknowledges that adjustments may be necessary along the way. Pivoting within the 15-year plan framework means having the courage and foresight to recognize when a change is needed and taking decisive action to redirect your efforts.

To effectively make pivotal course corrections, it is important to establish checkpoints or moments of evaluation along the way. These checkpoints serve as opportunities to assess progress, measure outcomes, and determine if adjustments are necessary. Here are some key considerations and indicators that can guide individuals in deciding when to correct their course:

Performance Misalignment: If performance indicators consistently fall short of expectations or desired outcomes, it may be an indication that adjustments are needed. Evaluate whether there are gaps between current performance and the desired trajectory towards long-term goals. Recognize when the current strategies or actions are not yielding the expected results and consider making changes accordingly.

Changing External Factors: Keep a close eye on external factors that can influence the feasibility or effectiveness of your current approach. Market trends, technological advancements, regulatory changes, or shifts in customer preferences can all impact your journey towards long-term goals. Regularly assess the relevance and suitability of your strategies in light of these external factors. If they significantly deviate from your initial assumptions or plans, it may be time to course correct.

Feedback And Lessons Learned: Actively seek feedback from mentors, peers, customers, and stakeholders. Their perspectives can provide valuable insights that help identify blind spots and potential areas for improvement. Pay attention to recurring feedback or patterns that suggest the need for adjustments. Additionally, reflect on the lessons learned from failures and setbacks, using them as guiding principles for making informed course corrections.

Evaluation Of Risks And Opportunities: Periodically evaluate the risks and opportunities associated with your current path. Assess whether the risk-reward balance remains favourable or if there are emerging opportunities that could significantly impact your long-term goals. Be open to considering alternative paths or strategic shifts that align better with the changing landscape or offer greater potential for success.

Self-Assessment And Personal Growth: Engage in regular self-assessment and reflection to evaluate your own growth and development. Consider whether your skills, knowledge, or mindset are evolving in alignment with your long-term goals. Be honest about areas where personal growth or professional development is needed and be willing to make adjustments to enhance your capabilities.

Incorporate these considerations into your approach, individuals can effectively monitor their progress and make timely course corrections. The key is to remain agile, adaptable, and receptive to change throughout the journey. Iterative course corrections enable individuals to stay on track, leverage new opportunities, and navigate challenges with resilience and perseverance.

It's essential to be open to new possibilities and to recognize that change is a natural part of personal and professional growth. Honestly evaluating your current situation, gives clarity on whether a pivot is necessary to align your trajectory with your evolving aspirations.

Reflection also provides an opportunity to assess the risks and benefits of a potential pivot. You have to consider the potential challenges and uncertainties that may arise from making a significant shift. You need to understand the potential impact of a pivot on your long-term goals and the feasibility of achieving them through a different path. This introspection will help you make a more informed decision and prepare yourself mentally and emotionally for the changes ahead.

Research And Exploration

Research and exploration play a crucial role in the process of pivoting within the frameworks. They provide you with the necessary knowledge and insights to make informed decisions about the new opportunities or paths you are considering. Conducting thorough research and exploring various industries, markets, or areas of interest will help you gain a deeper understanding of their potential and relevance to your long-term vision.

Here are some key steps to consider during the research and exploration phase:

Identify Areas Of Interest: Begin by identifying the areas or industries that align with your new direction. Consider your passions, skills, and values to pinpoint the sectors that resonate with you. This could involve exploring fields that are related to your current expertise or branching out into entirely new areas.

Gather Information: Dive into the wealth of information available to you. Utilize online resources, industry reports, books, articles, and professional networks to gather insights about the industries or paths you are exploring. Stay updated on the latest trends, market conditions, and key players in those fields.

Evaluate Fit: As you gather information and insights, evaluate the fit between your skills, interests, and the opportunities or paths you are considering. Assess how well they align with your long-term vision and goals. Consider the growth potential, market demand, and personal fulfilment that each option offers.

Experiment And Test: If possible, consider engaging in smaller-scale experiments or projects to gain hands-on experience in the areas you are exploring. This could involve volunteering, freelancing, or taking on part-time roles to test the waters and validate your interest and aptitude.

Continual Learning: Commit to continuous learning throughout the research and exploration process. Stay curious and open-minded, seeking out additional educational resources such as courses, workshops, or certifications that can enhance your knowledge and skills in the areas you are considering.

Remember that research and exploration are ongoing processes. Stay adaptable and open to new information and opportunities that may emerge during your journey. Regularly revisit and refine your research as you gain deeper insights and clarify your goals.

By conducting thorough research, exploring various industries or paths, and seeking guidance from mentors and experts, you can gather the information and knowledge needed to make well-informed decisions about your pivot. This research and exploration phase sets the foundation for a successful transition and increases your chances of finding a new path that aligns with your long-term vision within the 15-year framework.

Pro Tip: Force Majeure

You will undoubtedly encounter moments that are beyond your control, where unforeseen and uncontrollable events or circumstances disrupt your journey towards your long-term goals. Force majeure refers to unforeseen and uncontrollable events or circumstances that may disrupt our journey towards our long-term goals. Whether it's divorce, illness, or other life-altering events, remaining resilient and persevering through these challenges requires understanding and applying the principles of force majeure.

Force majeure events demand flexibility and adaptability. As you encounter unexpected changes, it becomes necessary to adjust your plans and expectations, understanding that life may not always unfold as initially envisioned.

While force majeure events can be overwhelming, they also present opportunities for personal growth and transformation. Through self-reflection, finding meaning amidst adversity, and seeking personal empowerment, you can use these experiences as catalysts for your development. Take on board the lessons learned and see challenges as opportunities, you can cultivate resilience and continue progressing towards your long-term goals.

In the face of force majeure events, prioritizing self-care becomes paramount. Taking time for self-reflection, engaging in activities that bring you joy and relaxation, and maintaining your physical and mental well-being are crucial aspects of navigating through these challenges. Practice mindfulness, seek professional help if needed, and nurture your emotional and physical health, to navigate the ups and downs with greater strength and stability.

Recognizing and embracing unforeseeable events like divorce or other life-altering situations is a critical aspect of your journey. It's okay to acknowledge your emotions, grieve, and heal; it's a human response. But remember, it's equally essential to balance emotional resilience with the determination to adapt and keep moving forward. Your long-term well-being depends on this delicate equilibrium.

Amidst these unforeseen events, support becomes an invaluable lifeline. Surrounding yourself with trusted friends, empathetic family members, or supportive groups can offer the stability and comfort you need during these trying times.

Developing a system in preparation for probable force majeure events into your 15-year plan equips you with resilience in the face of uncontrollable circumstances. Flexibility, personal growth, self-care, and seeking support become your allies in navigating challenges. These tools empower you to emerge from adversity even stronger, wiser, and fully prepared to seize new opportunities on your journey

Chapter Summary

In the final chapter of the 15-year plan, "Navigating Setbacks," we guided you through the process of overcoming obstacles and maintaining a resilient mindset. As you reflect on your journey towards achieving your long-term plan, it is essential to remember that setbacks are merely opportunities to get better aligned with your vision.

As you encounter setbacks, resist the urge to get caught up in the moment. Instead, maintain a calm and composed demeanour, keeping the bigger picture in mind. Remember they are temporary roadblocks, and your ultimate destination is still within reach.

Setbacks can be painful and disheartening, but they are transient. Recognize that the pain you feel will subside, allowing you to regain your focus and motivation. Treat setbacks as valuable learning experiences that propel you forward rather than hold you back.

The pursuit of knowledge and personal growth is an ongoing journey. Even in the face of setbacks, continue to learn, refine your skills, and evolve as an individual. Embrace a growth mindset that perceives setbacks as opportunities for improvement and development. Failure does not define your journey. It is the ability to bounce back from failure, learn from your mistakes, and adapt your approach that determines your success. Embrace failures as valuable lessons and steppingstones towards achieving your long-term goals.

The lenses through which you view the world shape your perception of setbacks. Fine-tune your lenses to provide a clear and objective vision. Challenge negative lenses such as self-doubt, blame, perfectionism, fixed mindset, and catastrophizing. By doing so, you cultivate a resilient and positive outlook that propels you forward.

As you reach the end of this book, celebrate your achievements and acknowledge the growth you have undergone throughout the plan. You are equipped with the resilience and clarity of vision to overcome setbacks and seize future opportunities.

Remember, setbacks are not roadblocks; they are opportunities for growth and self-discovery. By embracing resilience, maintaining perspective, and refining the lenses through which you perceive setbacks, you can navigate the challenges of the 15-year timeline with unwavering determination and a clear vision of your ultimate success.

CONCLUSION

As we conclude this book, you stand on the threshold of this grand adventure. Armed with newfound knowledge and a toolbox of strategies, you're now ready to craft the masterpiece that is your life.

When you first glimpsed your 15-Year Plan, it might have resembled Everest itself, with a summit veiled in the clouds of uncertainty. Yet, it was never about conquering an unscalable peak; it was always a profound journey with a clear path waiting for you to discover it.—a route paved with self-discovery, growth, and transformation.

Throughout these pages, you've embarked on a path of self-awareness, unravelling the intricacies of your current self and mapping a route towards the person you aspire to be over the next 15 years. The frameworks and insights you've gathered serve as guiding stars, illuminating your way to personal and professional fulfilment.

Time is a relentless force, and so much unfolds in the space of a year, let alone 15. This is your moment to seize the driver's seat, to set your destination to a place of your choosing, and to take the wheel of your life's journey. Along this path, savour each step, for life is not solely about reaching the summit but about relishing the moments, both big and small, that grace your voyage.

As you venture forward into your odyssey, embrace the challenges, celebrate the triumphs, and stay hungry for the extraordinary experiences that await. Your journey is your own, a canvas upon which you will paint the masterpiece of your life. With the tools, knowledge, and unwavering determination you now possess, your future is an unwritten epic waiting for -your pen to script its remarkable chapters. May the path ahead be filled with fulfilment, purpose, and the profound satisfaction of a life well-lived.

AFTERWORD

Closing the final chapter of 'The 15-Year Plan' marks the beginning of your immersive journey towards realizing your dreams. But this isn't the end; it's just the start. Our commitment to your success extends beyond these pages. We have prepared a comprehensive support package, including an array of tools, templates, documents, Excel spreadsheets, and video content, all meticulously designed to empower you on your path to personal and professional growth.

What makes these resources truly valuable is their versatility. You have the freedom to customize and adapt them to your unique goals and ever-evolving circumstances. Your 15-year plan is dynamic, and our resources are here to evolve with you. Our Excel documents offer in-depth tables and trackers, enriching your planning and monitoring processes.

Your journey is personal, and helping you achieve your vision is our mission. We are dedicated to being your steadfast companion, offering continuous support, updated materials, and fresh insights to fuel your pursuit of success. So, as you move forward, keep exploring, keep planning, and keep dreaming because with these frameworks in 'The 15-Year Plan,' your future is brimming with purpose and accomplishment.